SeX PiSTOls

THE MAKING OF

THE GREAT

ROCK 'N'

ROLL

SWINDLE

ALSO AVAILABLE IN THIS SERIES:

The Making of *Scarface*
The Making of *Taxi Driver*
The Making of *Raging Bull*

SEX PISTOLS

THE MAKING OF

THE GREAT

ROCK 'N'

ROLL

SWINDLE

JOEL McIVER

The publisher wishes to thank the Book Division at Lasgo Chrysalis London for their ongoing support in developing this series.

Published by Unanimous Ltd.
Unanimous Ltd. is an imprint of MQ Publications Ltd.
12 The Ivories, 6–8 Northampton Street, London, N1 2HY

Printed and bound in France

ISBN: 1 903318 84 X

1 2 3 4 5 6 7 8 9

Picture credits:
Cover: © Kevin Cummins/Idols.
Picture section: page 97 © Michel Linssen/Redferns; pages 98–99 and page 100 (top) © Ian Tilton/Retna; page 100 (bottom) and page 101 (top) © Paul Slattery/Retna; page 101 (bottom) © City Life, Manchester, www.citylife.co.uk; page 102 (top) © Ian Tilton/Retna; page 102 (bottom) © Ged Murray/Rex Features; page 103 (both) © Ian Tilton/Retna; page 104 © Brian Rasic/Rex Features

contents

Introduction   7
The most hated man in Britain   9
Producing the swindle   53
Kill your idols: scene by scene   79
The movie that would not die   127
Appendices   163
Index   203

introduction

In 1980, the Sex Pistols were on their way out. Their bass player was dead. The singer was broke and trying to forge a new career. The others were yobs at large. Their commercial popularity was on the wane and the public were sick of their endless, puerile spite.

One thing remained to them, however—one vital, last piece of groundbreaking controversy that would record for posterity the band's by-now hackneyed trademark stance, the lip-curled V-sign in the face. A movie, *The Great Rock 'n' Roll Swindle*, which would present an image of the Pistols to the public which served only the ends of its creators and which paid scant respect to the actual truth. Knowingly ironic two decades before that particular approach became culturally ubiquitous, *Swindle* took the Pistols—minus their singer John 'Johnny Rotten' Lydon who had wisely scarpered before shooting commenced, their manager Malcolm McLaren, a skeletal cast of support actors, and a new director, Julien Temple, to a different plane: the plane of artistry.

The Great Rock 'n' Roll Swindle doesn't make for easy viewing, though. Cobbled together by Temple—then an inexperienced beginner—from various ideas and fragments made during a succession of false starts, the movie suffers from an incoherent structure. This gives it a certain charm, though, and definitely sets it within the punk movement: a movement fuelled like no other by consequences-be-damned energy. Writing a book about it is no simple matter—the holes in the film are both frustrating and integral to its identity—but nonetheless a book is what it deserves. *The Great Rock 'n' Roll Swindle* is a British institution, revealing much about the flaws and the genius of its home country, as well as how impossible it is to categorize, define and thereby kill off the punk scene that spawned it.

One caveat. This book isn't a biography of the Sex Pistols or of the punk movement—both stories have been told exhaustively elsewhere—but an understanding of a film and its unique relationship with its creators and its audience. There's enough inside the movie to fill several books such as this, depending on how much the reviewer makes of its context and its implications—let alone the phenomenal degree of change instigated by its subjects. It's that kind of film.

Punk, however you understand it, is still around and relevant today—whether you interpret the word as a yellow-and-pink montage of newspaper print or as the spirit of rebellion for its own sake. The life expectancy of the kicking, screaming, musical infant born around 1976 is impossible to predict, but books like this are one way of judging its progress. Keep turning the pages.

Joel McIver, 2005
www.joelmciver.co.uk

the most hated man in britain

"We never sat down and wrote a thesis. There's no rules, and no order. We just do it, which is more to the point. Do it—and when you can't do it no more, then don't do it at all"

John Lydon

In retrospect, *The Great Rock 'n' Roll Swindle* shouldn't have been possible to make. When it started shooting in August 1978, its subjects—the Sex Pistols and their hangers-on—were in a state of chaos, and when it was distributed and shown in cinemas in 1980, it didn't reflect much of the state of flux that had surrounded the Pistols two years previously. That is, if you discount the grooming of Sid Vicious for a solo career. But what it did reflect was the magnitude of the storm of controversy that the band had ridden since their formation in 1975 and their rise to prominence the following year.

It's quite a story. Consider the following…

The Cast

John Lydon

In summer 1978, ex-Sex Pistols singer John Lydon announced the formation of a new band, Public Image Ltd, with a show of bravado, making sure that everyone knew how distanced he now was from his old band. However, underneath it all he was battling nerves and insecurity, as he would confide many years later.

"The Sex Pistols was a legacy. It was a serious problem to have to deal with at the time about what I would do next," he said. "I didn't want to do anything like the Sex Pistols, and Public Image just came around really very naturally from just hanging around with [bassist] Jah Wobble and [guitarist] Keith Levene. It just fell together... We never really discussed [the music] much before we went in, we just chucked it all at once on the table, and worked it out that way. But that nervous energy and doubt and fear of your own capabilities is what makes it, and absolutely no conceit towards following a genre."

Despite the success of his previous band, Lydon was also struggling with finances. "Money was a serious problem too... but do you know what? The lack of money and backing from anybody is what made it work. It made us try harder... I mean, nobody had anywhere to stay. My name was taken off me. Malcolm [McLaren, Pistols manager] claimed that he owned the rights to the name Johnny Rotten. He tried to stop us working—it was absurd. When things are like that, don't wallow in self-pity, get revengeful, and you get revenge by moving on."

Lydon's anger towards his former manager stayed with him for many years. In 2005 he said, "That man never helped me none. He never made my life comfortable. I've taken severe hidings and knifings while he ran and hid. He never helped us out. He never kept us together as a band. He never even kept us together as friends. He set one off against the other. Lies were the order of the day. He kept us all confused. How we managed to do what we did is utterly beyond him. Our own sense of unity and purpose is what kept us together."

Where this strength came from is evident: the singer's background had been a tough one. When Malcolm McLaren recruited him to the Pistols in 1975, Lydon—fresh from a semblance of Catholic-school education—was full of venom towards the system that had rejected and tortured him. As he told the *NME*'s Charles Shaar Murray, "Everything was taught in a very strict style, in the same way that they taught religion: this is the truth, the whole truth and nothing but the truth, and if you don't like it you're gonna get caned. But Catholic schools build rebels: a lot went along with it, but a lot didn't. There was always a riot in religion classes."

Elsewhere he explained: "I got kicked out when I was nearly 15—14 and a half—because I had too long hair... I waited a year and a bit because I went on building sites working, and then I went to get some O-levels because I still had it in me that O-levels were the way to heaven—plus I didn't want to work no more. I got a grant. It was very easy. For some reason I always liked technical drawing and geography. At college, I did maths, English, physics, technical drawing and chemistry... English Literature was a joke. I passed that with flying colors without even trying. It was stupid fucking Keats poetry, because I did my English in Catholic school. They kicked me out halfway through the course because they said I'd never pass, but they'd already entered me, so I went and took the exam privately, because I was still entitled to, down at the County Hall. And I passed with an A—and I went down there with the certificate and showed it to them."

His schooling had been grim, he said. "It was in skinhead times and they couldn't understand how a skinhead could like The Velvet Underground. It was quite apt. I went to the Catholic School in Caledonian Road [London], opposite the prison. What a dungeon!... it was terrible. They really destroy you with what they do to your soul. They try and take away any kind of thought that might in any way be original. You know when caning was banned? In Catholic schools, that didn't apply because they're not state-run. They get aid from the state, but they're not entirely state-run. I don't know where they get their money from... I'd like to know. It's probably some Irish Mafia. What they try to do is turn you out a robot. When it comes to allocating jobs for a student who's about to be kicked out into the wild world, it's always jobs like bank clerk... railroad attendant or ticket collector. Even the ones who stayed on for A-levels."

Lydon was also famously disgusted by the tail-end of the hippie movement, which was ebbing away as the Pistols stepped up to take its place. But—no fool he—Lydon admitted there were some truths behind the washed-out mantras that had become associated with that particular scene.

"It's very easy to fall into these hippie bullshit phrases, because some of them were good, some of them actually meant something. It's just a shame that they ruined a lot of them with silly ideas about 'Yeah man, I wanna be free,' which meant fuck-all. I can remember going to those concerts and seeing all those hippies being far out and together, maaaaan, despising me because I was about 20 years younger than they were and having short hair. That's when I saw through their bullshit. A lot of punks are like that as well, which makes me really sick."

So sick, in fact, that by the time *The Great Rock 'n' Roll Swindle* was released. Lydon was a long way away from the punk scene that had formed him.

Sid Vicious

As Lydon worked in secret on the band which he would shortly unveil as Public Image Ltd, the future was uncertain for Pistols bassist Sid Vicious (born John Simon Ritchie; he later changed his name to Simon John Beverly). Holed up in New York with his girlfriend Nancy Spungen (who Motörhead singer Ian 'Lemmy' Kilmister once described to the author as "terrible… if Sid hadn't knifed her I would've strangled her myself"), Vicious was being groomed from afar by manager McLaren as a solo star in his own right.

The reasons for this were clear. While Lydon had been the face, the voice, the creative force and the intellect of the Sex Pistols, Sid had won his own fanbase thanks to his combination of awkward charm (Lydon said the 'Vicious' tag had been applied in irony to this rather gentle man) and dark, nihilistic, vitriol. As Sid once put it: "We're quite nice, friendly chappies really, but everyone has a beastly side to them, don't they? I can't think of anyone I know who, if somebody messed around with them, they wouldn't do 'em over."

"When they push you into a corner like that, what are you gonna do?" Lydon added. "You either kill them or give up, which is very sad, because we're fighting people who ought to be on our side... or *are* on our side, but don't know it. They say we're using them, but the real people who are using them they don't even know about."

The question of Sid's ongoing relationship with Nancy was key to what would happen.

"Nancy came to England with the express wish, much like a groupie, to bed a Sex Pistol," recalled Pistols associate Pamela 'Jordan' Rooke. "And in a way, Sid was easy meat… Everybody wanted to be with Sid, but unfortunately he came with Nancy. She was unbelievably thick-skinned, one of the most unlikeable people I've met. Everybody could see through her—except Sid."

She added of the pair: "Sid didn't have any normal, ordinary, relationships, and I think the sex part overtook him. I always saw him as being the child to Nancy as mum. She was one of those doting people, and he had never had that in his life." As band photographer Dennis Morris also wrote, Lydon "would plead with [Sid] to get rid of her, but to Sid she was like a crutch. When they were together he was like a kitten, but without her he would go crazy."

In retrospect, Sid was a pawn: the *Swindle* was an alternative future for him which never happened.

The other Pistols

When Malcolm McLaren recruited Pistols guitarist Steve Jones, the latter was a petty criminal who had developed an antipathy to working for a living. As he said with some justification, "I didn't wanna work… it's pointless. I used to work as a window cleaner. Worked my arse off. Then you got paid and went out for a drink and blew it all in one night. Totally pointless." He once claimed to have stolen his guitar ("It would have taken too long to save up for it. And it's more exciting to steal"). Punk music was his passion: "I think the

New York Dolls turned me on to it. I saw them supporting The Faces and I'd never seen anything like it. Musically they were bad, but really exciting, really mad."

Drummer Paul Cook had played in a band with Jones, while original bassist Glen Matlock knew McLaren from the latter's shop, Sex. Matlock had a background in classic English pop that served the band well in composing terms but was soon used against him. As he recalled, "When I was a young lad, they had this thing called pirate radio in England, because national radio was such crap at the time. All these stations [were] on boats offshore, just outside the government's jurisdiction. It was all bands like The Kinks, The Who, The Small Faces, The Yardbirds and The Rolling Stones. We were kind of beginning to think about picking up the guitar and what kind of trousers to wear and your hair and 'My Generation' and 'You Really Got Me.' As I got older, one of my favorite bands was The Faces. That was the common ground between me, Steve and Paul. They were into The Faces and so was I."

Much later on, Matlock would say: "I left because me and John didn't get on, basically. Steve Jones and Paul Cook had a band in '72. I joined them, Steve was the frontman and then decided he didn't quite have it as a singer, so we was on the lookout for someone else and we got Rotten. I was the only one out of the lot of us who went to art school [St. Martin's]. That was one of the reasons we didn't get on, me and John. I think he was jealous, but he was quite a good painter, funnily enough."

The Bromley Contingent

If you were a music fan at this point in British history, times were hard. As Marco Pirroni—once of Adam & The Ants and all-round punk scenester—once explained, by the mid-1970s the glam-rock scene was dead and there was a musical vacuum.

"1972 to 1973 seemed to be really buzzing," he said. "It was only that lull of 1974 to 1975 that left space for things like punk to come through. 1974 to '75 was fucking dead. It was like that period when Elvis goes into the army, Chuck Berry's arrested, Buddy Holly's dead and there was nothing happening, then The Beatles came through. Roxy Music had split up, Bowie's just released *Pin-Ups*, Lou Reed had done *Berlin*, which now I think is a great album but then it was just dreary. Iggy was... fuck knows where he was—that was it, there was nobody else!"

Enter the Bromley Contingent, the key Pistols hangers-on.

A key member of this inner circle from their earliest days was Pamela 'Jordan' Rooke, who had been sporting a cropped punk hairstyle, plus 'punk' garments such as rubber stockings, since the age of 18. She lived on the south coast and would commute by train every day to work at McLaren's shop, Sex: "I used to have so much trouble on that train from Seaford, where I used to live," she recalled. "People used to swear at me, abuse me, the lot. I wouldn't take any shit, though, and on one occasion I threw a tourist's camera out of the train window. He flipped! Eventually British Rail had to give me a first class carriage to myself... I'd been dressing like that for ages, so punk wasn't a new thing for me. My mother had found me uncontrollable since the age of seven: through choice I had absolutely no friends at school—the clothes were an expression of that chaos."

She added: "Malcolm McLaren was always very interested in how people looked, and I loved everything that Sex was about... Malcolm, Johnny Rotten and I were very close. Johnny always tells the story of how he went into Sex one day—I had on this T-shirt with a big rip right across the front, so I'd put in a safety-pin to cover it up. Johnny thought it was great, and the safety-pin thing started there and then."

When, in 1978, the NME's Julie Burchill asked her: "Why do you choose to look like you do?" Jordan replied that it was a way of life. "Why did Picasso paint? I always looked weird. My mother always told me I was repulsive... Not everybody can do a job they enjoy, and I loved it there. I believed in the things that Malcolm and Viv were doing." After a fashion report in Honey in 1976 that read "Go down to Sex, if not for the clothes then just to see the strange girl inside," Jordan became almost as well known as the band themselves.

Julien Temple
McLaren's employment of Julien Temple as director was significant. The young film-maker—then a student at the respected National Film And Television School—had first encountered McLaren in 1975, when Temple was filming scenes of the punk movement with a camera illicitly borrowed from the School. As he recalled, "I had been filming The Clash before the Pistols, and used to go into the 100 Club with the camera. Malcolm didn't like his band being filmed, though." Nor did the owners of the punk clubs: Temple and his friends used to smuggle the camera into the club in pieces—shell, lens and so on—and then re-assemble it in the toilets.

McLaren caught Temple doing this and, reasoning that if Pistols footage was needed, it would be better to recruit someone who was already making it, employed Temple as an archivist on £12 per week—"probably more than the Pistols themselves were making at the time," the director said later. For the next two years Temple faithfully tracked down and stored as much Pistols footage as possible. It would be needed...

Malcolm McLaren and Vivienne Westwood
Malcolm McLaren was, like so many self-styled Svengali pop managers, a former art student and aesthete. When—at the ripe old age of 30 in 1977—he was interviewed about the young band he had assembled the previous year, he told the press that he'd lost interest in popular music after the impact of Beatlemania in 1964. In his twenties he had settled into managing clothes shops with various fashionable (or at least fashion-aware) themes. One of these was a King's Road establishment called Let It Rock, which specialized in 1950s-style rockabilly outfits.

As the artist Jamie Reid—soon to become a crucial Pistols accomplice—later said of McLaren's frequent proclamations that he invented punk: "He's wrong, because the most important people are always the punters. I know it's a cliché, but it's about the people on the streets, because that's where real life is, and where all the real ideas always come from. He was just in a position to put the ideas out."

Of McLaren, Steve Jones stated: "He's our manager, that's all. He's got nothing to do with the music or the image...he's just a good manager".

As McLaren's then-partner, the well-known clothes designer Vivienne Westwood, later explained: "The teddy boys hung out in the shop, and soon we started to make clothes for them. First the designs were unisex, and then we created clothes for women and young girls. We based the look on rock 'n' roll right from the beginning. Even though it was the 1970s, we found old stocks of clothes that had never been worn from the 1950s and took them apart. I started to teach myself how to make clothes from that kind of formula.

"In the 1980s, the shop lease was up and I didn't know whether to renew it. By that time I saw copies of my clothes on the Paris catwalks. I had to think about what to do. We didn't have much money, but I knew I had ideas. I thought it would be stupid to stop. I was still interested in the youth rebellion but nevertheless I stopped being a victim, stopped trying to attack the establishment, realizing that it takes too much of your energy."

The punk look came about when "we wanted to step off our island and add the colour of the Third World. We got gold cigarette paper and stuck it around our teeth. We really did look like pirates and dressed to look the part... I was the first person to have a punk rock hairstyle... I've had an awful lot of influence on make-up. I would have liked very early on to have had financial backing and help with production—but it didn't exist in England."

"We hated the older generation," she said on another occasion. "It wasn't young people, but old people we felt were responsible for the mismanagement and cruelty in the world still going on. It didn't stop when Hitler killed himself. To us, it was a way of saying to the older generation: 'We don't accept your values or your taboos.' Really throwing it in their face: 'We are what you are.'

"The key word to me is 'destroy.' What I realised from my experience of punk rock was that the idea of destroying something doesn't mean anything. Not only that, it might even be harmful. I don't believe in this 'destroy' any more. I believe in ideas: the secret is education. The world could change. What I learned from punk rock was that you don't change the establishment by attacking it. In the case of punk, it's just an idea that could be marketed. Punk was a marketable commodity. At the same time was the pretence that we have free expression. I did not want to be a token rebel. I just went faster. You need ideas."

The History

The Plot Thickens:
What Happened After The Pistols And Before The Swindle
The Sex Pistols played their last show together on 17 January 1978 at San Francisco's Winterland Ballroom. It was a sprawling, lacklustre, performance that ended with John Lydon's much-quoted taunt, "Ever get the feeling you've been cheated?" The group's manager, Malcolm McLaren, had instigated and nurtured tensions between the band members to the point where the atmosphere had become unbearable and, disillusioned by their lifestyle and the industry, they went their separate ways in late January.

Lydon, the sharpest and canniest Pistol, flew to New York, where he busied himself with preparations for a new project. Sid Vicious stayed in Los Angeles for a while before following Lydon to the East Coast on 20 January. He suffered an overdose of methadone on the flight and was admitted to

New York's Jamaica Hospital on arrival. The plan formulated by McLaren was that Vicious would join Jones and Cook on a trip to Brazil, but this never came to pass.

Journalist Roberta Bayley tracked Vicious down at his bedside in hospital and asked him what had happened. The weak Vicious, who she described as lonely, bored and anxious to talk, explained the overdose with the words: "What happened was, I done 80 milligrams of methadone, right?... and about six or seven Valiums—and when you get high in the air it has a much greater effect on you than it does when you're on the ground. You know how you get pissed a lot quicker in the air? So that's what happened."

Asked about the status of the Pistols, Vicious mused: "I left them... I don't think anybody really wanted to continue, but no one had the guts to actually say it. So I just phoned John up and told him what I thought of him and where I thought he was at...

"I still think I'm pretty good. I think I was better than any of the others. [Steve and Paul will] probably try and get another band together and fail. John's completely finished. I'm hoping [this will] shake him up and then he'll be able to do something—that'd be good if he could do that. But otherwise if it doesn't shake him up and get him out of it, then as a person, not only will he not do anything, but also nobody will even want to know him. They'll say, 'Oh, didn't you use to be Johnny Rotten?' I'm glad that it's over now because it was like... I feel like I was the only one still putting any real energy into it. Did you see our show at Frisco? I mean, John wasn't doing very much, was he?"

As for himself, Vicious seemed locked into an addiction that he couldn't, or wouldn't, shake off. "The doctor said that if I drank anything like vaguely remotely like the way I've been drinking for the past... however long, that I've got about six months at the absolute outside to live, and like the drugs as well, so I more or less can't do anything. If I went out anywhere I'd just like... sit there. If I went out anywhere I wouldn't be able to resist the temptation—that'd be the trouble. Like, I'd end up just boozing myself out."

When Bayley asked him if he planned to clean up, he complained: "I can't straighten up. I just can't be straight... I suppose I just have to. I haven't figured out yet quite how I'm gonna do it 'cause I haven't been straight in like four years. I had hepatitis and when I got out of hospital I fucked myself up as badly as I could. I don't know why, but everybody said you can't do it, so I just went ahead and done it. It's my basic nature. My basic nature's gonna kill me in six months."

Vicious' weakened state was a pretty good metaphor for the overall status of his band: lost, desperate and short of options. But fate—or at least his manager—was working on his behalf.

Far from closing the door on the Sex Pistols, McLaren, always one step ahead with his plans, had been laying the groundwork for a Sex Pistols film. When Steve and Paul landed in Brazil, their first move was to visit the Great Train Robber Ronnie Biggs, who had been living in Rio de Janeiro since fleeing the UK in 1963. Despite having taken place 15 years earlier, the enormity of the robbery was still vivid in the British public's minds, and while 'celebrity gangster' culture may be very fashionable nowadays, at the time the meeting was judged to be in shockingly bad taste. McLaren sent a film crew, headed by novice director Temple, to record the meeting and the subsequent months that Biggs and the two Pistols spent together: Cook and Jones would not return to the UK until March.

So much for the end of the Pistols. But what of their earlier days?

The Rise To Filthy Glory

In 1974 McLaren was stunned by the arrival at his store of the American proto-punk band the New York Dolls, whose "humanity and musical ordinariness" impressed him sufficiently to make overtures to them on a business level. Obviously struck by this persuasive Englishman, the Dolls took McLaren on as their manager back home in America. One of his more interesting moves during this temporary post was to incorporate the symbol of a Communist hammer and sickle into their live show, a provocative idea in the Cold War 1970s. Fuelled by his experiences with the Dolls, he renamed his shop Sex on returning to the UK. Leather, fetish and S&M clothing was now the order of the day.

McLaren had learned a lot from his brief time in the US, telling *Sounds*: "The trouble with the Dolls was that their hype was so much bigger than they were. They really had an opportunity to change it all around, but instead of ignoring all that bullshit about signing up with a company and a big advance, they got sucked in…

"They [bands] get dazzled by the process. Every time The Ramones have a picture of them published it lessens their mystique. There's no mystery about the New York scene.

Pretty soon Richard Hell is going to leave the Heartbreakers and Sire Records will dangle a contract in front of him and he knows it won't help, and won't do any good, but he'll sign it because it's what's expected of him."

Toying with the idea of assembling a band of his own, McLaren began looking around for suitable candidates. A regular at Sex was John Lydon, then 19 years old, who wore inventive apparel such as an entire suit ripped apart and re-assembled with safety pins. "I liked his taste in clothes," McLaren told *Rolling Stone*. "He'd never sung before but I thought, he looks like a really disagreeable fucker—maybe he's the right guy."

It was quickly apparent that Lydon had talent. Some theories attribute his formidable live presence to the famously intimidating 'Rotten stare'; some go deeper. Clash bassist Paul Simonon once said: "John seemed like he had a pretty strong attitude towards the audience—or anybody— in so far as it wasn't 'Pleased to meet you, this is my little group' and more a case of 'I don't give a toss about you. I'm on the stage and I'll do what I like.' If you think about that period, most of the world was still in flares and had long hair, and here's this character with a ripped-up jumper and cropped hair.

"The first time we had a conversation was outside the Screen On The Green [in Islington, London] and he was with a bunch of his mates. I went over and asked him if he knew where I could buy some cigarettes and he said 'Yeah, there's a shop about two miles in that direction.' We giggled at each other, he showed me the shop and it went from there. I haven't seen John in ages, but we seemed to have a respect for each other from the start. We both came from non-musician situations, which might have something to do with it."

By late 1975 Lydon had been added to Jones, Cook and Matlock (the bassist worked at McLaren's shop) and the band was up and running. It should be noted, however, that all the Pistols have publicly disputed McLaren's role in the founding of the new band. Matlock, for example, once remarked: "Malcolm's full of shit, to be honest. I mean, he tries to paint it that he created us [and that] the songs were nothing to do with the success, but that was bollocks. You can't hoodwink people like that."

By early 1976 the Sex Pistols were playing self-composed songs such as 'I'm A Lazy Sod' and 'I'm Pretty Vacant' [sic], rather than the old Small Faces and Who tunes that they had used as a training template. McLaren began booking them live dates such as art-school balls, avoiding the usual pub circuit. "I didn't want them playing to 25-year-old beer drinkers who wouldn't give them the time of day unless they were playing Chuck Berry songs," he said. "I wanted a fresh, untainted audience."

"The trouble with the pubs," he added, "is that they're free, and people come for that reason. If you're at a Sex Pistols gig you wanted to go, because you spent money to get in. I opened the shop because I wanted people to make a certain statement and they wore my clothes. The Sex Pistols are another extension of that."

The audience he craved came rapidly out of the woodwork. Young music fans—sick of the sterile mid-1970s music scene—adopted the look, the jargon and the wrathful, bitter attitude of the early punk scene with amazing speed. The confrontational look that we now recognise as punk was in place by autumn 1976, typified by Nazi symbols and insignia, rubber and bondage wear, and mild self-mutilation. Chains and safety pins were a favored punk stamp.

Middle England held up its hands in horror as a wave of new bands—The Damned and Siouxsie & The Banshees among them—formed what we now know as punk's first wave. Lydon, however, was not impressed with what he saw as "departmentalisation". "It's the wrong thing to do," he sneered to the author in 2005. "It's *music*, mate. I bought music long before I became 'a punk person' and a long time after!"

Violence at the gigs and in the attitudes and soundbites of the bands became common. The optimistically titled Festival Of Punk Rock took place at the ever-liberal 100 Club in London in September, but was cancelled after one day when an audience member lost an eye after a beer glass was thrown.

Asked about the violence, McLaren ruminated: "It's been overstated by the media. But what violence there is, is genuine. The business has taken music away from these kids and they're trying to seize it back."

Ah yes—the business. The industry. The establishment. The system, which was the punk movement's enemy of choice from the moment it began and the enduring target for almost all the bile its musicians had to offer over the next few years. While the idea of the kids versus the business wasn't a new one—hadn't the hippies been protesting with that very idea a decade before?—this time there was a more tangible focus. Rather than the general repression by authoritarian parents, teachers, cops, military, government and the corporate world that had fuelled the Woodstock generation's ire while Lydon *et al* were schoolboys, the 1976 punks had more specific enemies.

By December it was clear who the Pistols' first enemy was: the record company who had first signed them. Perhaps the conservative giant institution EMI should have listened more carefully when McLaren crowed to the press: "The thing to do is just ignore [the industry]. No one came to sign up The Rolling Stones, no one wanted to know. But when they saw a lot of bands sounding like that, with a huge following, they had to sign them. Create a scene and a lot of bands—because people want to hear it—and they [the record companies] will have to sign them, even though they don't understand it."

McLaren had planned well. The actual signing of the deal with EMI seemed to be based on genuine enthusiasm from the younger, lower echelons within the company. EMI chief of A&R Nick Mobbs, who signed the Pistols, had the awareness to say: "The fact that many of us are now over 30 means we don't have our finger on the pulse. We have to question the whole idea of rock music and what it means."

McLaren had come to EMI after turning down three other offers and being turned down in return by big players such as CBS, whose A&R manager Dan Loggins had a rethink later on, saying: "I don't see why [punk] shouldn't be as revolutionary as San Francisco in the 1960s. It's gonna give the business the kick up the arse it needs. The question is, what happens to the revolutionary stance if these bands do have success? The music business is notorious for co-opting revolutionaries into the establishment. Look what happened to Dylan..."

McLaren commented: "I thought the only way to get the band credibility was to sign with the one company every journalist was going to hate and the whole industry was going to be amazed by. It's turned everything upside down—EMI spending £40,000 on a band who can't even play the 100 Club... But if we do get a hit record it's going to blow the whole scene wide open. Labels are going to have to say, 'Whether we like it or not, we've got to get involved.'"

Typically, the Pistols brazened it out when they entered the lion's den. On walking into the EMI offices, Lydon commented, "What a fuckin' dump." A nearby executive responded with alacrity, "If you don't like it, you can fuck off," but despite this initial skirmish a two-year deal was signed.

But the Sex Pistols' relationship with EMI would be short and painful. Having signed to the label on 9 October for £40,000—a sum that raised eyebrows at the time, having been somewhat inflated by the band's live reputation to date—the band were initially welcomed, trumpeted by a spokesman with the words: "They've got to happen for all our sakes."

After two recording sessions with producer Dave Goodman and then EMI staff producer Mike Thorne, the Pistols settled on Chris Thomas for the recording of their debut single, 'Anarchy In The UK,' released on 26 November and made Single Of The Week by *Sounds*. (The Damned had released their 'New Rose' on 5 November, thus laying claim to the first punk single.)

This fighting talk of 'anarchy' might have seemed merely rhetorical had it not been for the occasional statement that emanated from the Pistols' coterie. Consider this later thought by Vivienne Westwood: "It seems to be that liberty is reduced in direct relation to that in which organization increases... unless governments are willing to function in an environment that allows people to think, we won't have ideas. This is why in the past, the French governments have had people smashing the windows on the Champs Elysées, because they allow their people to think, unlike the British public school system. Anarchy is dangerous, of course, although I am not an anarchist. It does not mean to say that I believe in any sort of anarchist government. Individual liberty does involve anarchy—governments have to allow a certain amount, otherwise people don't think. The answer lies in education. We're being trained up as a bunch of consumers rather than thinkers."

Rumor had it that the music on 'Anarchy In The UK' had been recorded by a gaggle of progressive-rock musicians. Steve Jones spat in response: "Of course we did [play it]. Everything else is a lie. Do you really think Chris Spedding, John Wetton and Bill Bruford could have played like that?"

So far so good, then, despite a much-quoted 29 November live ban at Lancaster Polytechnic, thanks to local authorities who allegedly refused to entertain "that sort of filth in the town limits." But it was the infamous appearance on 1 December 1976 on Thames TV's *Today* show, hosted by the long-time presenter Bill Grundy, that brought the Sex Pistols to truly national prominence and dealt the fatal blow to any future relationship with the deeply traditional EMI.

The *Today* show has been widely quoted, correctly and otherwise, but for the record the key elements are Rotten's muttered throwaway line of "That's just their tough shit" (to which Grundy insists, "What was the rude word?... Good heavens, you frighten me to death"), the presenter's goading of Siouxsie Sioux ("Are you worried, or are you just enjoying yourself?… We'll meet afterwards, shall we?") and Jones' deliberate "You dirty sod. You dirty old man!… You dirty bastard!… You dirty fucker!… What a fucking rotter!"

Bill Grundy signs off with "I'll be seeing you soon, I hope I'm not seeing you [the band] again. From me, though, good night."

It was indeed good night from Grundy, who was regarded as having incited the Pistols to swear. He was suspended for two weeks after the show and his contract was not renewed the following year. His TV career dried up in the early 1980s and he died after a car crash in 1993.

Most observers couldn't understand why Grundy, a respected broadcaster, would push the band to swear. He himself offered no explanation, but Glen Matlock—in his autobiography, *I Was A Teenage Sex Pistol*—explained it thus:

"I met a journalist in my local [pub]. He'd known Grundy through work—or the Fleet Street grapevine. His version of that evening was that Grundy hadn't wanted to interview us. It wasn't because he thought the show shouldn't do anything on punk, but that he didn't know enough about it himself and felt someone else should do the interview. Or perhaps he just didn't think we were worth giving the time of day to. After all, he was the very first man to interview The Beatles on TV. He must have considered us well beneath him.

"It turned into a control-room power struggle. He felt that if he didn't want to do something he shouldn't have to do it. His idea was that he should have last call on what was on the show. His producer saw it differently. He laid it down to Grundy the way it was. Which was: 'Do it or get out—I call the shots in here.' There was a face-off in the control room and Grundy lost. By the time he went on air he'd already had enough of it. So he vented his frustration on us. Frankly, he couldn't give a damn about anything at that point. Plus he'd obviously had a few."

Matlock also added a postscript: "Funnily enough, I did see him one more time. It was about six months after I left the Pistols... We happened to drive past the Thames TV studios, and Bill Grundy came out of the building. It was the middle of the day but to me it looked like he'd just cleared his desk out, ready to leave for good. He had a briefcase in each hand and bundles of papers under each arm.

"The car stopped at the lights and we gave him a right ribbing—'Oi, Bill, remember me?' He stared at me and obviously did... he stood there on the kerb eyeballing us. Then he carefully put down his briefcases and papers and looked to the left, looked to the right and looked behind him. Then he just went, wallop, giving us two fingers with each hand. At last he'd been able to tell the Pistols to fuck off."

The day after the broadcast the tabloids were in a froth, with the famous headline 'The Filth And The Fury!' emblazoning one particular red-top. There was also the case of the enraged viewer, a lorry driver, who—in a spectacular example of infantile idiocy—put his foot through the screen of his brand new TV.

EMI gave a collective shudder of horror and at their Annual General Meeting, six days after the *Today* show, EMI chairman Sir John Read addressed the shareholders with the following words.

"During recent years in particular, the question of acceptable content of records has become increasingly diffIcult to resolve—largely due to the increasing degree of permissiveness accepted by society as a whole, both in the UK and overseas. Throughout its history as a recording company, EMI has always sought to behave within contemporary limits of decency and good taste, taking into account not only the traditional rigid conventions of one section of society, but also the increasingly liberal attitudes of other (perhaps larger) sections of society at any given time.

"It is against this present-day social background that EMI has to make value judgements about the content of records in particular. EMI has on a number of occasions taken steps totally to ban individual records, and similarly to ban record sleeves or posters or other promotional material which it believed would be offensive.

"The Sex Pistols incident, which started with a disgraceful interview given by this young pop group on Thames TV last week, has been followed by a vast amount of newspaper coverage in the last few days.

"Sex Pistols is a pop group devoted to a new form of music known as 'punk rock.' It was contracted for recording purposes by EMI Records Limited in October 1976—an unknown group offering some promise, in the view of our recording executives, like many other pop groups of different kinds that we have signed. In this context, it must be remembered that the recording industry has signed many pop groups, initially controversial, who have in the fullness of time become wholly acceptable and contributed greatly to the development of modern music.

"Sex Pistols have acquired a reputation for aggressive behavior which they have certainly demonstrated in public. There is no excuse for this. Our recording company's experience of working with the group, however, is satisfactory.

"Sex Pistols is the only 'punk rock' group that EMI Records currently has under direct recording contract and whether EMI does in fact release any more of their records will have to be very carefully considered. I need hardly add that we shall do everything we can to restrain their public behaviour, although this is a matter over which we have no real control."

Stern stuff from Sir John, but not, it appeared, an attitude which was wholly shared across his huge company. Mike Thorne, the aforementioned staff producer, told one interviewer that the Bill Grundy incident had actually gained the Pistols support in certain quarters of EMI.

"There was a big shift in support on the shop floor within EMI, completely towards the group. This august institution hadn't had as much fun in years, and it was exciting even for the most reserved employees to be connected to something which was clearly noteworthy and making big waves... The senior management, however, took a different approach. They were part of the establishment which the group was baiting, and a connection with the Pistols would not help progress towards a mention in the Honors List."

In due course, EMI dropped the band, who left in gleefully high spirits at the amount of cash they had been paid for so little work. Thorne continued: "When the group was dropped, the workers were disgusted. What were we doing trying to find and develop bright new and novel acts when one of the most promising in years was kicked out by the bosses?...I considered resigning, but realized that it would accomplish nothing: they were gone, and the regime would not change its attitude."

The aftermath of the Bill Grundy incident would have pleased a modern-day record company no end. Despite a protest by EMI factory staff when asked to handle the record (which rather contradicts Thorne's claim that shop-floor support went to the Pistols) and the BBC scarcely acknowledging the record's existence, the 'Anarchy' single sold 1800 copies the day after the show. The first concert of the forthcoming Pistols, Clash, Damned and Heartbreakers tour—due to be held at the University of East Anglia—was cancelled by the vice-chancellor on the grounds of 'public safety.'

More bizarrely, before being allowed to play in Derby, the Pistols were commanded to play a set in the judge's chambers before members of the Derby Borough Council Leisure Committee—to allow those selfsame members to decide if their act was suitable or not. The band refused and another date was cancelled. As McLaren remarked, "Obviously, we're not going to submit to that sort of censorship. If we did, it could set a horrifying precedent which other bands would have to follow."

As the band climbed aboard the coach which would take them to the next stop on their tour—Leeds—Lydon gave the V-sign to a nearby crowd of reporters, accompanying it with a shout of "You fucking cunts!"

"These kids," sniggered McLaren, "really don't give a fuck who hates them."

The Pistols' reputation was spreading internationally by this stage, especially in America, which had a punk movement of its own. Ramones manager Danny Fields remarked that he "hadn't seen any safety pins through nose or cheeks or ears at CBGBs... When we do, we'll know British punk has arrived." It wasn't long until this happened, though, with 1977 as potent a year for the band as 1976.

From 30 years' distance, it's easy to conclude that the Sex Pistols simply ricocheted from disaster to public outrage to disaster again, with their career—on paper, at least—one long series of incidents. But remember that this was a rock band—whatever tags you placed on their music—locked into the same process of 1) signing a deal, 2) recording an album, 3) touring and promotion, 4) return to 2) as every other commercial outfit.

In the case of the Pistols, though, there was the context—late 1970s Britain, a country that seems to have been grey and culturally dormant. It wasn't that it was producing no art or music at all, but those who lived through this era do tend to agree that—just as there is an economic cycle with periods of low growth—the UK was at a low point in terms of new artistic ideas. This is why the Pistols contrasted against the background so starkly, and why any movie made about them must, if it contains any truth at all, be a similarly gripping experience.

So, when the band were reported in the press as having "spat, vomited and sworn" in the terminal building at Heathrow on returning from a five-day tour of Holland on 4 January, the public were aghast. Nowadays, this would hardly merit a mention in any but the most conservative of publications. The irony—of which there is so much in this tale—is that the story was never proven to be true. Other sources suggest that the band bypassed the main terminal building and that an EMI staffer escorted them every step of the way. And McLaren had experienced a similar event when he was managing the New York Dolls. Could he have fed the same story to the papers with his new band?

True or not, it was the last straw for EMI, who terminated the Pistols' contract on 6 January. The big-selling 'Anarchy In The UK' single was still being pressed due to public demand, but orders from above saw production cancelled immediately. Later in the month the company agreed a settlement figure of £20,000—all for a band who had recorded precisely one single.

McLaren didn't hang about. Three days later he was in the office of Derek Green, managing director of A&M Records, playing him a demo of 'Pretty Vacant,' 'No Future,' 'No Feelings,' 'Submission' and three versions of 'Anarchy.' He also met Jerry Moss—the M of A&M—in Los Angeles to discuss the band's American future.

More turbulence awaited. While McLaren was in the US, Sid Vicious—then merely a friend of the band's—did a phone interview for LA radio. During the conversation he said that he had been 'auditioned' by the Pistols, although they had a long-standing and competent bassist in the form of Glen Matlock, composer of many soon-to-be-successful Pistols songs.

Famously, Vicious couldn't play bass but—establishing a punk trademark in doing so—the Pistols recruited him anyway, with Steve ostensibly giving him lessons. Incapable as a musician he may have been, but he certainly had strong opinions. On the subject of music journalists, he told the writer Judy Vermorel not long after he joined the band: "They're just so thick they wouldn't know a string quartet from a string vest. They're just totally dumb. They don't know a fucking thing. They just make me sick. They make me physically ill, because they're not in touch with what's going on. They've got no idea of what's happening. And they can't, you know, they can't handle it...

"As soon as somebody stops being a kid, they stop being aware. And it doesn't matter how old you are. You can be 99 and still be a kid. As long as you're a kid you're aware and you know what's happening. But as soon as you 'grow up'...

"I've got absolutely no interest in pleasing the general public at all. I don't want to, because I think that largely they're scum and they make me physically sick, the general public. They are scum. And I hope you print that. Because that is my opinion of like 99 per cent of the shit you find in the street who don't know a fucking thing."

Vicious immediately made an impression, telling the media in a mixture of sarcasm and amusement: "I hate the name Sid. It's a right poxy name—it's really vile. Rotten started it. He's horrible like that, he's always picking on me... I stayed in for about two weeks because everybody kept calling me Sid, but they just wouldn't stop... I'm a highly original thinker, man, he's just jealous because I'm the brains of the group. I've written all the songs, even right from the beginning when I wasn't even in the group. They was so useless they had to come to me because of they couldn't think of anything by themselves."

Of the Pistols' fanbase, Vicious also crowed: "The trouble is that the general public is so contrived themselves that they can't imagine how anybody else could not be contrived. Therefore, if you're not contrived they've got to find some way of justifying their own contrivance."

As Lydon told John Tobler of *ZigZag* in April 1978, the bassist's nickname came from "Syd Barrett of Pink Floyd fame, [and] we called him Vicious 'cos he wasn't vicious, he's just a big baby who eats sweets. Look at him!"

Tobler responded, "I thought you called him Sid because there was an albino hamster that you had both owned?"

Vicious came back: "Yeah, that *was* called Sid. I hated the name. I was always going on to John about how I hated the name Sid, so he started calling me Sid to all my friends. I made the big mistake of denying it, and I was Sid for ever after, so I thought, 'I'm stuck with it now so I'd better like it.'"

On McLaren, Vicious was hard to pin down, commenting, "He was a miserable little artist from the East End with pretentions of being middle class. In his closet in Clapham he's got this ridiculous picture of an awful load of scribble and it's meant to be a chair... and there's Vivienne squawking away in the corner sewing things up, babbling away to herself. I hate her as well... we like them. They're our friends. Where would we be without Malcy-Walcy?"

Lydon said of his newly recruited friend: "If you want to know how I first found out about Can, it was from Sid! And I don't mind telling anyone that, 'cos that's the truth, that's how we were with music. We'd all go out and find our things, and you might not like it, or you might, but that's what it was about. And all of that seems to have gone now. It's now all about imitating something and the older it is the better, and the less anyone knows about it the more fashionable it makes it. Well, I don't think so...

"I've always been very open about the music I listen to. It's extensive and huge—I don't have any limitations. Alice Cooper has always been in there, but journalists don't want to hear that. I even have Val Doonican records, and why not? I like some Genesis very much, I can't remember which one now, but I do! Peter Hammill—my God, that album *It's Over* is fantastic! He's just moaning and groaning away. His wife ran off with his best friend and it's really sad! But I loved the way he dealt with it emotionally: he just got angry with them, instead of self-pity, so I respect it.

"Yet I'm supposed to not like stuff from that class structure. Wrong! I like people from any structure when they are honest. I liked Joy Division at the time, very early lot, and all that nonsense about the singer killing himself was like well, 'how fashionable, but how stupid'!"

As for music, Vicious affirmed a view which has been endlessly repeated ever since: "What I want to do is put something else out that I like, and, like, whoever else likes it will find it—do you know what I mean? And, like, if nobody else in the whole world likes it, I couldn't give two shits. If it doesn't sell one copy, who gives a fuck? The point is that it's what *we* want to do. We have fun making it. We have fun listening to it. I listen to our records a lot because I like them. I think they're good records, otherwise I wouldn't have had any part in them. I like our music to listen to as much as I like The Ramones to listen to... I'm incapable of doing something I don't want to do. I just can't do it. I can't force myself to do things. I either want to do it or I don't."

Vicious was a fascinating character. He had been brought up in the south of England by his mother, Ann Beverly, who had had some problems with heroin herself. As Pistols photographer Dennis Morris later wrote, "Deep down he was a shy person... I think he was frightened of the audiences. Sometimes he showed no emotion at all." A man with much to offer the Pistols' ever-more-erratic cause, then, and when he was formally recruited on 28 February, McLaren sent a telegram to the British music papers to inform them of the change in line-up.

This was followed by a new record deal with A&M, whose executives McLaren had clearly impressed. After the actual document was signed on 9 March, a photo call was organized for the following day at the gates of Buckingham Palace, where the event was re-staged for the benefit of the press.

In July 1977, Steve Jones told Sweden's *Expressen* newspaper that Glen had been replaced with Vicious because "Glen liked The Beatles... the rest of us hate The Beatles. And it turned out he loves them. He came up with all these Beatles-influenced chords and melodies that I couldn't play. Besides, we didn't really get along either. Sid's always been around the band."

Contrarily, Jones admitted to liking more than a few classic rock acts: "Who *did* I like? Yeah, The Faces. The Faces were always fun, always did a good show. But look at Rod Stewart today. He makes me sick, he's a fucking cabaret artist. Yeah well, the New York Dolls of course. And The Doors, mainly Jim Morrison. And Iggy's *Raw Power*."

In 2004 Jones finally admitted to a taste for mainstream AOR, saying: "Journey's great. Back then I couldn't like it because it wasn't cool. When you get older, you just appreciate a good song, whether you're wearing flares or bondage pants. I love catchy pop-rock. You can't knock a good song. But on my first day, if I would have played Journey, I think I would have buried myself."

Lydon was clearly unaware of Matlock having been ousted for his Beatles preferences, saying in 2005: "No, that's silly press nonsense. Although Steve might have said it... he's a bit of a dummy. Glen was very much a Beatles fan, but he's also a Kinks fan, and they wrote some of the greatest lyrics ever written. And The Small Faces too, they were a hilarious band live. Just fantastic energy, although I never liked it on record. I liked Rod Stewart live very much when he went solo, but he was much better in The Faces."

Much later, Lydon pinpointed the removal of Matlock as the indirect work of McLaren: "Me and Glen were set up against each other. Our arguments have been much reported on—and badly reported on!—but we were both lied to. We've sat down and talked about this since. Malcolm told me that Glen wanted the band to be like The Bay City Rollers, right? No, Glen didn't want that, but that's what Malcolm told me, and I believed him and didn't bother to question Glen about it. And I should have done. Now, what is a grown man doing that to us for? What's his motivation, other than some kind of sicko spite and jealousy? He wanted to divide and rule, because he's talentless."

Asked at the time if all the controversy the Pistols had generated in recent months was "an artificial creation of the record industry", Jones sniggered: "That's the most stupid thing I've heard. How the fuck can they say that? Don't they know anything? It's just the opposite. They wanted nothing to do with us, they were scared of us. We're the opposite of the industry darlings like Queen. Shit, you can't even dance to Queen... and that pompous singer..."

The band's violent image was "exaggerated by the press," he added. "It's a fucking joke. I can't believe it—no one gets it. The violence and the swastikas is a joke to shock people."

As for Lydon, he revealed something of his intellect—and his awareness of where his band stood culturally—when he told writer Sture Johannesson in 1977: "We are total English working class. None of us have had what you could call an education. Because in Britain you don't get one unless you have rich parents or know the right people. We're the first rock movement, since I suppose the 1950s, not the 1960s. The 1960s had it very easy. It was like Swinging London, you know, money was all over the place. We're much, much closer to early rock 'n' roll. That's where our energy comes from. It's the same kind of energy, except that our songs aren't about Long Tall Sally. They are about being bored to death, nothing to do, nowhere to go after 11 o'clock when the pub's closed.

"In England they don't like you to be entertained, because it means your brain would begin to think for itself and this they don't like. That's why they are trying to stamp out the punk movement. Because it's a whole generation thinking about everything. We are about making people think for themselves once again—if they ever did. Just get up and do it. If you feel like you want to be in a band, you should. When we started, it was impossible in England to play in small clubs. Rock music had died and we started it up again."

But he knew his limits as an activist, musing: "You see, I'm in a rock band, I'm not a politician. What I am about is just letting people live the life they lead. Don't judge people by their clothes, but by what they do... I never judge people ever by their clothes. Our audiences in England are widely different. We get all of them, the lot, every kind of person. And that's the way it should be. It's not just about people who come in a safety-pin jacket and stuff... It is just to make people happy about music, it's to be excited to sing in a live band. I mean, it is an exciting thing, it is a good thing, it's fresh. It is real, it doesn't come straight out of a studio... You should be given the chance. I hope we do give them a chance... And people say that we are negative. I think we are totally positive. There's nothing negative in what we are doing. It is negative if they don't accept us without even hearing us."

But Lydon knew that his band had a platform that had to be used, and was eager to exploit that—in his own obvious intention, despite the anarchic spiel—for the common good. "We don't set out to provoke society, we set out to do what we want to do and say what we say without people interfering: you should be allowed free speech. After all, England claims it's democratic. I think we have proved that wrong, it is not. It is a very, very controlled state."

The members of the establishment who had feared the band from its outset had done so, he reasoned, "because they were all to some extent slightly controlled by the industry. There was always an element of the establishment behind it, but with us it's totally our own. We do what we want to do and there's no industry behind us... They can't control us, we're uncontrollable. They've predicted all down the line against us, and they've failed. This scares them. They've never been able to do that before. They've always known before that the money would come into it, but they've missed the boat so many times."

Power—true power—as he saw it, lay with the fans. "The kids are the ones who make all the decisions now," he said, in contradiction of the later iconoclasm of the *Swindle*. "They're the ones that count, and I hope they've got the brains to suss it all out for themselves and not be told by the press 'This band is finished' and then think, 'Yes, that's right, they're finished and I'm not going to like them any more. I'm now going to like this.' They've got to decide for themselves."

Lydon had enunciated the key point of punk: that getting involved was the idea. As film-maker Don Letts explained, "You have to understand, punk rock was not a spectator sport! In the beginning, punk was not a fan thing by any means, it encouraged you to get up, get involved, and do your bit. That much was fundamental, almost a prerequisite demand made on you. It followed an ethic of 'a good idea attempted is infinitely better than a dull idea perfected,' so all my friends and contemporaries were out there, picking up guitars, and I'm like 'Whoa, the stage is full, but I wanna get on this ride, man', you see? Of course I didn't have any formal training. At that time I didn't *want* any formal training—I was following the punk rock vibe of just get up, get out there, and do it! That was our culture, so it was then I reinvented myself as Don Letts, the film-maker."

The originality of thought that went into the first wave of punk was also of paramount importance if the music was to make any impact. "Let me quote Orson Welles to preface my views," Letts added. "He said to aspiring film makers, 'Look, if you want to make a truly original film, don't watch any more films!' Can you appreciate where he's coming from?

"For me, I just kicked off, rolling film in the heat and sweat of The Roxy, but as I did more and more, shot more and more film, I came to understand the importance of being rooted in the discipline of learning a craft. Then there is the artistic process: what justifies you in picking up a camera in the first place? Are you aware, *deeply* aware, of what constitutes good picture composition and framing of your subject? So yes, I am aware of a deep duality present within me, because I know there is also great deal to be gained from the kind of blind 'fuck you' energy of just going out there and doing it, without any preconceived notions or value structures. I work with that dichotomy all the time."

Tessa Pollitt, bassist of The Slits, added: "Punk was about doing your thing, creating your own thing. It wasn't about being a follower; it certainly wasn't about being some kind of punk stereotype. It was about creating your own thing. When all the followers and clichéd bands started, I just thought, 'What the fuck are you doing? This isn't what it's about.' We always carved out our own path, strove for something fresh and new."

Asked how many truly original bands there were in the punk scene, Lydon later mused: "Quite a few, actually. The Adverts were always up there. You could put Gary Numan's Tubeway Army in there too. The Raincoats, for introducing a violin into it. X-Ray Spex I love for Poly Styrene's voice and the saxophone. But when you say 'punk', what do you mean? Because at the time you had The Police, too. And The Jam.

They'd all fall under that banner. Labels bugger us all up. And you're implying that nothing happened before punk, and nothing since. You've fucked it with that attitude straight away."

More establishment-baiting took place three days later, when the band were part of a skirmish at the Speakeasy Club with 'Whispering' Bob Harris and his engineers on BBC2's *The Old Grey Whistle Test* TV music show. One of the presenter's companions required 14 stitches in his head after an unidentified member of the Pistols' entourage hit him. This led to a solicitor's letter to A&M's Derek Green, who talked to the company's founding duo, Jerry Moss and Herb Alpert. Rumor had it that pressure on the Pistols also came from Peter Frampton, one of A&M's top signings, who shared management with Harris, but this was never confirmed. Whatever the truth, A&M dropped the Pistols midway through production of their next single, 'God Save The Queen,' after a few promo pressings had been manufactured: today these fetch over £5,000 in mint condition.

The months of filming that lay ahead were presaged in late March, when a Pistols show at Leicester Square's Notre Dame Hall, owned by the Roman Catholic church, was filmed for a documentary by a camera crew from the US NBC channel. This was followed by a short break for the band in Berlin and more filming on their return—this time by Don Letts for his *Punk Rock Movie*.

The publicity was good so far into the new year, but the record company situation was less promising, especially after a rejection by CBS. The only large player left was Richard Branson's relatively new Virgin label, which had spent the last four years building its profile according to the semi-hippie, semi-progressive instincts of its founder. While Vicious was hospitalized for a bout of hepatitis, Virgin announced that they had signed the Pistols.

As with EMI, some of the manufacturing staff got cold feet about working with this most controversial of bands and pulled union strings to make their feelings heard. On 17 May staff at the pressing plant refused to make the new single's pressing plates; the next day the sleeve artwork plate-makers refused to co-operate—both groups were placated. Ten days later the single, 'God Save The Queen', released to tie in with the Queen's Silver Jubilee for maximum controversy, finally appeared.

Its iconic artwork, designed by punk artist Jamie Reid, made an instant impact. Virgin promoted the release with its biggest advertising campaign to date. The BBC instantly banned it from airplay, stating that it was "in gross bad taste," and the Independent Broadcasting Authority issued a warning to all radio stations that the single could be in breach of Section 4:1:A of the Broadcasting Act.

But perhaps McLaren's finest hour as manager of the Sex Pistols came on 7 June, the day of the Silver Jubilee, when much of the nation was sipping Double Diamond or Babycham at street parties celebrating 25 years of the monarch's reign. The Pistols, their manager, associated hangers-on, press and Virgin staff—about 200 in all—hired a boat (yes—the *Queen Elizabeth*) for an evening sail down the Thames, with the band performing the song as the boat passed the Houses Of Parliament. With events such as this going down in history, how could a film of the band *not* be made?

The boat trip went well until its end, when it docked amid a crowd of waiting police officers. Julien Temple's camera crew was ready and waiting, but the confrontation was slow to build. When it came, it came quickly, with 11 arrests—among them McLaren for 'using insulting words likely to provoke a breach of the peace', Vivienne Westwood for 'obstructing a policeman' and artist Jamie Reid for assault.

All the arrested parties pleaded not guilty at the magistrates court at Bow Street and were remanded on bail. The real impact was felt when 'God Save The Queen' stormed up the singles charts to number two—a fitting aftermath to the boat debacle. *Sounds* magazine stated: "There is little doubt that it was the fastest selling single last week, but the fact that several of the 'chart return' shops had banned the single kept it from the number one spot." It also quoted a Virgin spokesperson as saying "If it does get to number one, then it will prove the much-vaunted power of radio and television is negligible if the public interest is already there."

This view wasn't shared by DJ Tony Blackburn, who said of 'God Save The Queen': "It is disgraceful and makes me ashamed of the pop world but it won't last." (To which Virgin quipped, "As for Tony Blackburn, he makes us all ashamed. But he is a fad that won't last.") A group of cross-party MPs also tried to get the single banned. Virgin's spokesperson commented: "It is remarkable that MPs should have nothing better to do than get agitated about records which were never intended for their Ming-vase sensibilities. In fact, the record was broadcast last Saturday on Radio London by Charlie Gillett on his *Honky Tonk* programme—no one complained."

The biggest irony? 'God Save The Queen,' without a doubt the most lurid incident in the already colourful career of the Sex Pistols so far, was not destined to reach number one—that honour was retained that week by Rod Stewart's 'The First Cut Is The Deepest.'

As the single sold in droves, this irreverent cartoon-controversy turned nasty at one point. Lydon, producer Chris Thomas and studio-owner Bill Price were attacked by thugs outside the Pegasus pub. The singer's arm was slashed open and he was treated for tendon damage. In another incident, drummer Cook was attacked with an iron bar.

It seemed that despite their huge record sales, not all the public loved the Sex Pistols. Matters weren't helped by Malcolm McLaren's attitude to the press, revealed in a *Sounds* interview on 18 June. "We hate giving interviews for the purpose of giving interviews," he told Sandy Robertson. "There isn't any point. It gets a bit pointless: you end up losing not gaining, because you don't have anything to say. We don't want to talk about ourselves; if we talk about ourselves then it's only a star-conscious interview—it's not about something, a fact. We don't like doing interviews about ourselves."

Although he was in fact giving just such an interview, McLaren added: "I don't like kow-towing to music journalists, press… it only benefits a very minor section. Believe me, it's only a certain type of person who buys rock journals. A lot of kids who go out on the street and buy records never read rock journals, that's a fact. I tell you that 60 per cent of the records sold in this country, that portion of the public have never heard of the *New Musical Express*. And out of that 60 per cent, at least 30 per cent are young kids. So you've got your 30 per cent there who just hear something on the radio and say, 'That sounds good,' or they saw it on *Top Of The Pops* or

Saturday Scene. Or they saw their mate up the road looking strange with a record in his hand, so in order to be the second kid on the block, he goes and gets it. And that's how most records are sold and it's a fallacy to believe that they're sold in any other way."

McLaren had a mission, he explained: "I don't care if some university social secretary phones me up and says he played 'Anarchy In The UK' at his disco on Friday night, that don't mean nothin'... [but if a] 13-year-old kid who lives in the middle of Hampstead Garden suburb in a £50,000 house walks out and buys 'Anarchy' then that's doing something... I don't allow 'em to play universities for that same reason, there's no point, you just got a bunch of curiosity seekers, a few intellectuals."

He also had strong ideas about how to get that message across. "The record companies should be spending huge fortunes, not on taking out back pages in *Melody Maker*, but putting out TV advertising, because that's gonna get to 14-year-old kids. Bay City Rollers sold thousands and thousands of records; who is replacing them? What are those kids buying now? They're buying a bit of Sailor, they may be even buying Abba, they'll be buying some other thing that's Top Five... It's those kids that count... those are the kids you wanna change... you don't wanna play to university students."

Finally, McLaren's plan to make a film came out: "Well, the only concrete plan that's gonna happen... what I'm working on at the moment is TV and film. That has the potential of being seen by a lot of people who normally wouldn't... We can't play in this country properly, except for a couple of crummy universities, so I think it's better to have a film out. If you can have a film and it goes round the circuits and young kids say, 'Oh, let's bung in the back and see the Sex Pistols'—because they wouldn't be going to Southampton University but they can maybe afford 75p to go to their local [cinema]... If they see it there, then they're seeing it in a very good context."

And so back to where we started—1978. What could go possibly go wrong now?

1978-1979: The End Draws Near
Far from dropping the band concept after Lydon's departure, McLaren had big plans for the Pistols.

While in Brazil, Paul Cook and Steve Jones recorded two songs with Biggs on vocals, taking the idea of siding with a known criminal to a whole new level. One was the provocatively titled 'Belsen Was A Gas,' an existing Pistols song that was reworked for the purposes of the film. The other was titled 'No One Is Innocent—A Punk Prayer By Ronald Biggs' and was released as a single in June, despite Virgin's fears about the probable reaction. The UK 12-inch bore the slogan 'The Biggest Blow—A Punk Prayer By Ronald Biggs,' keeping fans and critics bemused as to its real title and just what the hell McLaren was playing at. All the balls were kept in the air by the B-side—Vicious' solo version of the Frank Sinatra staple, 'My Way,' on which he debuted his singing voice—much indebted to Rotten's nasal whine— with some extra semi-obscene lyrics.

On their return to Britain, Cook and Jones effectively found themselves as Pistols for hire. Despite nonchalant remarks such as "Ronnie Biggs was a right laugh. I'd like to do some more with him," guitarist Jones was battling a heroin dependency, but the duo still managed to record sessions with various punk and New Wave luminaries. The first of these was with Johnny Thunders, sometime New York Doll and newly solo recording artist. Alongside Thin Lizzy frontman Phil Lynott, Steve and Paul performed on five songs on Thunders' *So Alone* album for Real Records, including—with great irony—a song called 'London Boys,' a sarcastic response to the Pistols' own 'New York.' This was followed by live shows in London with Johnny Thunders' Allstars, and a guest spot for both men with The Clash at the Music Machine in Camden on dates in July.

All this activity was certainly keeping the idea of the Sex Pistols as a viable entity in the public's minds, or more accurately in the UK's weekly music press. A more significant live show came on 15 August, when the prepped-for-stardom Vicious performed what would be his only solo show in Britain at the Electric Ballroom under the name the Vicious White Kids. The line-up of this tentative new band was Vicious on vocals, Steve New on guitar, The Damned's Rat Scabies on drums, Nancy Spungen on backing vocals and—in another superb bit of irony—Sid's Pistols predecessor, Glen Matlock, on bass.

And so the die was cast.

producing the swindle

"We don't wanna do it"

John Lydon

Malcolm McLaren first conceived the idea of a Pistols movie as early as February 1977. Once he had hatched his idea in the midst of chaos—both planned and otherwise—the small task of writing, casting, rehearsing and producing it reared its head. Money was the first hurdle to be cleared, so McLaren began sending out feelers, at home and abroad. In June 1977 he set up a company, Matrixbest (after his music production company, which was called Glitterbest) to handle video releases as well as the forthcoming movie.

A radio interview, probably by a regional BBC reporter, quotes Lydon as saying that McLaren was in the US at the time in order to expedite the film. The singer said that the probable choice of director would be the cult director Russ Meyer, adding sarcastically that the movie would be "awful, terrible, hideous."

The idea of Lydon the urban prophet and Lydon the film star was one that some found hard to reconcile, and the singer hastened to pre-empt the predictable accusations of selling out with the words: "I hope people understand that it won't affect my lifestyle. I don't want to clothe myself in loads of money and hide away, that's not me. I couldn't live like that; I'd go completely insane from the bottom of it. If I ever did have a lot of money, the first thing I would do is

[buy] a recording studio and let new bands record there free, so they could hear themselves when they start. That is a good thing to do, I don't see why the Stones don't do that. They have the money—Led Zeppelin and all those bands, what do they do with their money? They don't help new bands. They should. That's music, that's what it is supposed to be all about."

Of the selling-out claims that would dog most of his career, he later told the author: "I'm always listening to that twaddle. Selling out what? The only thing I've sold out is venues, mate. Packed 'em to the rafters. This is the joke: I've never copped out on anything for the money. I have never ever sold my principles for cash. And I never will... I was accused of being a traitor and selling out for daring to like The Bee Gees. It's not an admittance, it's just a fact! Right? Fucking hell! I don't mean 'Staying Alive'—I mean the *real* Bee Gees stuff. All those mining disaster songs were so powerful. I know they're Beatles-influenced, but they took it a stage further."

Back in the BBC interview, Steve Jones interjects that the Meyer-directed film would be "really boring and dreadful... [but with] plenty of knockers." Thus he hit the nail on the head.

Russell Albion Meyer was born in March 1922 in California and learned his craft as a newsreel cameraman during World War II. After the war he worked as a glamour photographer for *Playboy* magazine, among others. This led naturally to a career as a director of erotic films, all charged with ribald content and revealing a fetish for the large breasts of the strippers and go-go dancers he recruited as actresses. His movies rapidly attracted a cult following, especially with the advent of the permissive society and improved filming technology in the late 1960s. Highlights of his filmography included *Faster, Pussycat! Kill! Kill!* (1965), *Beyond The Valley Of The Dolls* (1970, written with renowned film critic Roger Ebert) and *Beneath The Valley Of The Ultravixens* (1979). The last of these would in fact be his last movie (apart from a vacuous effort in 2001 with porn star Pandora Peaks), but in 1979 the Russ Meyer brand was at its peak—hence McLaren's interest. As a slightly controversial, very un-British candidate for director, it's easy to see why McLaren pursued his services—even if the band themselves (and especially Lydon, who by the end of the decade was starting to feel jaded) were less enthusiastic.

At this stage Lydon still seemed to be in favor of the forthcoming film, telling one interviewer: "We're gonna make a film. A proper feature film, since we're not allowed to play in England... We are gonna make a proper movie and have us playing live on the film and show around cinemas to people that can't see us normally. I hope it takes off...

"Russ Meyer, have you ever heard of him? Well, he's a loony. We only like people working with us who have a sense of fun. Some of the songs are really serious, but they have a moment of fun at the same time ... because music is for fun, not sitting down and being miserable... We have to break it all down, bring it back to reality. Just make people happy. I'm no superstar, I never will be. I'm just like anybody else."

One of the songs written for the movie soundtrack was 'Who Killed Bambi?'—a ludicrous, semi-music hall rant which would ultimately be performed by Ed Tudor-Pole, Pistols associate and punk 'face'. The song lent its title to an early version of the script, written by Meyer's collaborator Roger Ebert. Meyer is said to have agreed a directing fee with Matrixbest of £30,000, although this figure has never been confirmed.

Funding for the film came in October 1977 from Warner Brothers, who are reported to have committed £200,000 to the project as well as a further £50,000 for the US release rights for the forthcoming Pistols album, *Never Mind The Bollocks... Here's The Sex Pistols.*

Shooting actually began under Meyer's direction—a few minutes still exist in an archive—but after two days the project was cancelled. Possible reasons for this are many. One is that the funding was suddenly withdrawn, and another is that the studio concerned was too intrusive. The latter theory was borne out in an interview with Meyer (who died of pneumonia in 2004). "It wasn't really as rewarding as I thought it could have been," he told *The Onion.* "There was too much interference from the studio that we were working with, so it wasn't that keen a thing. That's all. It just didn't give me what I wanted, and Ebert felt very much the same way—that we were kind of pinned down."

Asked what he thought of McLaren, Meyer mused: "I think Malcolm McLaren needed at least one more lay in his life. I don't think he really understood much of what I was doing. Not that it was dreadfully important that he had to know, but he was obviously not in the same mold as me. He was always after me, trying to pick up anybody, even girls that were built like a willow, and so on. We weren't that keen on it."

He was much more enthusiastic about Sid Vicious, saying: "I liked him. I thought he had something going for him. I liked Sid Vicious. His problem, too, though, was a little too much with the whipping and that kind of stuff. It didn't go in with me, particularly."

Meyer also remarked that McLaren withdrew his support. "He just abandoned it! Roger did a great script. It's all so unfortunate. That experience drove me to not make more films for quite a time. It's depressing to have a project collapse like that. I traveled to New Zealand and Switzerland just to get away from it. McLaren, that is. It's damaging to have a project just drop like that."

Meyer's biographer, Jimmy McDonough, explained that the director had never been much of a rock fan, with his musical tastes going in other directions. "Music was definitely important to Meyer," he said, "but he cared little for rock 'n' roll, preferring the sounds of big bands and Engelbert Humperdinck. He just shared the same juvenile delinquent attitude. As well as a frantic energy… The Sex Pistols were a far different sort of entity.

"Would they have provoked Meyer to greatness or would he have reduced them to a caricature? Hard to say."

One voice not normally heard in the story of the Pistols' fiery demise is that of Julien Temple, the young man who—as the band's long-term archivist—had filmed the events of the Jubilee. At one point Temple even remarked how focused and positive the band seemed at the end of 1977. Their last UK show—a firemen's benefit on (of all days) Christmas Day—was a powerful statement of cohesion, and as they were about to fly to the US for a tour of small, Southern venues, many believed that the following year would be a great success for them. Yet within a fortnight the band had split up. How had this come to pass? "I feel Malcolm wanted to wreck it," said Temple.

Wrecked it certainly was. McLaren had chosen the US tour dates carefully, avoiding major, culturally savvy cities and concentrating on conservative ones where the Pistols would be guaranteed to cause maximum offence—Atlanta, Memphis, San Antonio—although this in itself wouldn't have been too much for the controversy-hardened band to handle.

But conflicting factors were at play. Lydon—the most jaded of the band, probably because he was the most intelligent—was being aggressively courted by Virgin as a solo star in his own right, with the record company implying that he was the real star of the Pistols and that it was high time he struck out on his own. McLaren, meanwhile, had his eye on grooming Sid Vicious for a solo career. Vicious, however, was struggling with heroin to the point where it hindered his already naïve bass-playing to a serious degree, while his on-off relationship with Nancy was aggravating his band mates. It was potentially explosive situation, and one that was bound to come to an end sooner rather than later. For the Pistols that end came in January 1978 in the Winterland Ballroom in San Francisco.

With the movie in tatters after the Meyer/Ebert fiasco, McLaren now had to rethink the script dramatically to take into account the episodic nature of the available footage. Some of the archive footage and the Ronnie Biggs material had been shot on tour—notably in San Francisco for the 'Ever get the feeling you've been cheated?' final show—and Brazil. But adding to his problems was the fact John Lydon was now no longer a Sex Pistol—and had made it clear that he would not be involved in the movie project.

The person McLaren finally chose as replacement director was Julien Temple. Only 24 years old when McLaren had first given him the go-ahead to begin filming the Pistols in spring 1977, Temple was a newcomer to directing, but he had studied at the National Film And Television School. What made him the perfect candidate was his art-school background (always related to the punk ethos in subtler ways than most observers realized) and his passion for the Pistols, whose music he had first encountered at college.

How Temple came to work with the older and famously manipulative McLaren on this project is in itself illuminating. As Temple put it: "It came about as most good things do, by default. Various projects fell through while I had been filming the Pistols. We thought we could piss off Sex Pistols fans with it."

So here's the first unique aspect of the motivation behind *The Great Rock 'n' Roll Swindle*: its makers actively wanted to alienate the fans who would pay to see it. Temple further explained this apparently self-defeating motive with the words: "The problem for [the Pistols] was that kids were worshipping them and kneeling down in front of large posters of them and praying. They were not meant to be worshipped, but meant to inspire people to get up and do a similar thing. The idea of the film was to knock that notion on the head and confuse truth and reality in an infuriating way so fans would get angry again."

Temple added: "It was made at a very different time with a very different purpose: specifically in the immediate aftermath of that band at that time, to display the aura of pop divinity as fake. You know, kids were idolizing them in the same unthinking way they idolized The Bay City Rollers or Rod Stewart in England. And *The Great Rock 'n' Roll Swindle* was meant to be kind of a mischievous joke, taking the piss out of this band that were supposed to be the saviors of the world at that point for a lot of kids. I think it was an important thing to do, questioning the belief in things that challenged you to question the belief in things in the first place."

Iconoclasm was the order of the day, and so McLaren and Temple set out to explode the myth of the Sex Pistols. That is, if there even was one: no doubt Lydon would have disagreed with the premise that the Pistols' fanbase had lost touch with its idols, who had always remained accessibly down to earth, and deliberately so. There are other implications, too: the act of disillusioning—and thus removing—a band's fans is anathema to most music managers. For McLaren to actively celebrate the idea was a new and disturbing concept, verging on nihilism. Nothing like this approach had been witnessed in cinema until this point.

In fact Temple had in fact been closely involved with the *Swindle* since the long months of setting up funding and casting in 1977. At the time, the director later recalled, he was living in an apartment in Marble Arch in central London, and McLaren would often visit the then-archivist in the evenings. Together the two would hack out ideas for the script, eventually landing on a workable structure that gathered together all the extant footage from TV and other sources as well as leaving space for the planned filming. "Malcolm played a large part in it," he explained, giving McLaren his due despite the personal friction that would follow. He also said that McLaren, despite his erratic nature, was in many ways a man of great talent—his almost Situationist approach was fascinating.

Situationism is—in this context at least—shorthand for the commodification or subversion of art, politics or experience in general. With hindsight, that's not a bad label to apply on McLaren's management practices, the motive for *The Great Rock 'n' Roll Swindle* and, indeed, the content of the film itself. "Everything the Situationists said in the 1960s became true," McLaren would say later. "When I helped put 'God Save The Queen' to number one and had it banned from the radio at the same time, [Situationist founder and chief writer] Guy Debord called me up on the telephone—I'd never spoken to him in my life—and said: 'Thank you very much for getting my record to number one!' As far as he was concerned he owned that record, and he owned that idea. And I thought, 'brilliantly audacious and truly wonderful,' and I never forgot it. I agree with him: it was his idea, yes!"

Temple's declared view was that a movie on the subject of the Pistols was not only a cunning move: it was actually expected. In the great tradition of rock movies—pioneered by The Beatles with *A Hard Day's Night* in 1964—and the mostly so-bad-they-were-good releases that followed, the public were ready for such a product. As he would explain later, movies from earlier in the decade by Slade (*Slade In Flame*) and Marc Bolan (*Born To Boogie*) had possessed a certain charm, despite their obvious limitations—but the filmic quality wasn't necessarily a priority. The simple fact of there being a film about 'their' group that an audience could go and see in a cinema was more than enough. Little wonder

McLaren seized the opportunity to recruit a film-maker so early in the process of making his band famous.

The solution at which Temple arrived was to structure the film in ten chapters, each headed by a 'lesson' from McLaren (styled The Embezzler in the movie) and consisting of extant footage or newly commissioned material. Each chapter leads off with McLaren explaining to his assistant, Helen Wellington-Lloyd (a dwarf and Pistols associate who went by the name of Helen Of Troy), the nature of each lesson. In adopting the episodic structure, Temple displayed a fair degree of wisdom for one so young. It's difficult to see how else the film could have worked, with the documentary-style footage that he was obliged to use.

Once Temple had assembled a script, based on the footage already shot and the archival TV film they knew they wanted to use, shooting new material could begin. The bulk of Temple's shooting took place in the spring and summer of 1978 at various locations in London, with one notable scene set at Marylebone station. Although Lydon was now absent, the other ex-Pistols went along with the project, as it offered a decent salary—and in Vicious' case, would serve as a useful springboard to a solo career.

As Steve Jones recalled, actually making the movie was chaotic to say the least. "It was done not like any other movies were done. We were just kind of wingin' it as we went along. There was no real script. It was fun. I enjoyed it, because it was kind of chaotic... I think it was mainly Julien who was kind of steering the ship. Of course, McLaren had some ideas, but it was Julien. I'd ad-lib on stuff I was doing as well.

"I regretted that Russ Meyer didn't do it, like he was originally meant to... I think it would have been good if them guys had done it. It would have been like more of a proper movie. More organized. And there would have definitely been a lot of birds with big tits. But I enjoy the outcome. It doesn't make any sense, but it's very entertaining..."

Asked if the film was nothing but a publicity exercise for McLaren—who practically hogs centre stage throughout—Jones reasoned: "I was so not concerned with all that. We all know what McLaren's like. Some of us accept him that way and some of us don't... I accept him. Because I've known Malcolm ages, before the Pistols ever started. If you believe all the stuff he says, then you're a fool. It's pretty obvious that he's full of shit...

"Malcolm did have some great ideas in the beginning. He's an egomaniac, you know. Unfortunately, he started believing his own bullshit. That was the downfall of him. He's never had a bad heart, though... He didn't take care of any business. It was all the other bullshit. Press, trying to scrounge up some media stuff. That was more what he was good at."

The rest of the casting was mostly a simple affair, although Marianne Faithfull—who Temple had originally wanted to play the role of Sid's mother—dropped out after doubts about a proposed sex scene. The role was then scrapped, with more focus put on Nancy Spungen as Vicious' on-screen companion in some scenes.

From three decades' distance, Spungen's few screen minutes are fascinating. 'Nauseating Nancy'—as the tabloids dubbed her for her publicly violent character—was 19 at the time of filming and had already gained herself a spectacular reputation. A troubled girl since her childhood in the middle-class Jewish circles of Huntingdon Valley, Pennsylvania, Spungen had been hyperactive as a child and had undergone therapy ever since. Depression and numerous suicide attempts in her teens had accompanied a career as a groupie, stripper and alleged prostitute after she moved to New York. She supposedly moved to London with the solo purpose of seducing a Sex Pistol (or, some have it, Jerry Nolan of the New York Dolls), and—as Jordan told us earlier—was introduced to Vicious through Lydon. The pair grew close, with the bond fuelled by the drugs they abused together, and the relationship rapidly became a threat to the future of the Sex Pistols. Ultimately it was one of the root causes of the band's split.

Another brief but entertaining female role in the *Swindle* comes from Mary Millington, the 1970s porn star who was—for a few years at least—famous for the ribald adult films she made. Ranging in degree from hardcore pornography to humorous *Carry On*-style softcore films, her movies were controversial and popular enough to make her an eye-catching addition to the cast list.

Another tragic figure to add to the list of those associated with the Pistols, Millington was born Mary Quilter in 1946. She embarked on a career in porn after a chance meeting with film-maker John Lindsay in the late 1960s. Lindsay cast her in *Miss Bohrloch* (ie 'bollock') in 1970 and she made a series of similar films over the next few years in parallel with a magazine career and a stint as a high-class prostitute. The publisher David Sullivan, with whom she had a long affair in the 1970s, elevated her to national fame through the pages of his adult-entertainment empire and films such as *The Playbirds* (1978) and *Queen Of The Blues* (1979). After repeated police harassment of the sex shop where she worked, Millington succumbed to depression, which manifested itself in kleptomania and drug abuse. On 18 August 1979, just a couple of months after shooting wrapped on *The Great Rock 'n' Roll Swindle*, she was arrested and told that in all likelihood she would be given a prison sentence. That night, at the age of just 33, she took her own life with a combination of paracetamol and alcohol.

Millington's biographer Simon Sheridan, who profiled her controversial life and tragic death in his book *Come Play With Me: The Life And Films Of Mary Millington*, says of her role in the *Swindle*: "Although Mary's role in *The Great Rock 'n' Roll Swindle* was explicitly sexual—she was only hired to play a girl shagging in a cinema, albeit one asking Steve Jones some very probing questions about his punk rock career—it was still a side step away from the 'sex comedy' arena and propelled her into something more 'respectable.' It was a different type of movie from her usual grind.

"Mary often joked that: 'I was born respectable, but I soon decided I wasn't going to let that spoil my life.' This was a fun soundbite from the queen of British sex, but she was actually born illegitimate, and throughout her life she actively sought respectability and normality. She wanted to be accepted so badly—by men, by society, by the film business. I honestly think she thought that by doing a film with this new, trendy director and the most famous British band since The Beatles, she was actually entering a new phase of her career. Sadly it wasn't to be."

Does Sheridan see any similarities between the situations of the Pistols and Millington?

"She was an ordinary working class girl who had, virtually overnight, become Britain's most notorious woman. The Pistols were the same—hyped up to a point of insanity. Everybody knew who they were, and the establishment hated them. It hated Mary Millington's sexual excesses and hated everything that punk rock stood for. Mary and the Pistols were excellent bedfellows. They just emerged from opposite sides of the same dirty bed sheet. I have no doubt that Mary was asked to participate in *The Great Rock 'n' Roll Swindle* because of her infamy."

How would her involvement benefit the movie?

"Mary truly was a box office draw, a bona fide *name* that would attract the punters. Getting paid £1,000 for her one-day shoot on the *Swindle* just cemented her reputation as an icon of late-1970s cinema. It was the easiest money she'd ever make in her relatively brief career, and having her name splashed all over a poster alongside the Sex Pistols was not going to harm either participant's reputations. Two rebels—the punks and the porn princess—together for the first time!"

But with that came a glimpse into the tragic side of notoriety too. By the time the Pistols' movie was released both Millington and Vicious were dead, both by suicide.

"In the end," Sheridan believes, "Julien Temple's film encapsulated the end of an era—farewell to the decadent, over-indulgent 1970s. With the deaths of Mary and Sid, it was suddenly goodbye to all that... It seems ironic that when Mary finally got some good reviews from a movie performance, she was sadly already dead. If she'd lived to see

The Great Rock 'n' Roll Swindle released, her life may have changed beyond her wildest dreams."

Another key figure is Edward Tudor-Pole, who sings 'Who Killed Bambi?' in a memorably over-the-top performance towards the end of the movie. In fact, Tudor-Pole was being considered as a potential replacement for Lydon at the time of production. Instead he secured rather more success with his own band, Tenpole Tudor, who scored a Top 10 hit with the excellent post-punk shoutalong 'Swords Of A Thousand Men' in 1980. A long period of public anonymity followed, although he kept gigging as a solo act. He returned to the limelight in the 1990s as a presenter for the *Crystal Maze* TV show, and he has also acted in films such as *The Rocky Horror Show* and Alex Cox films such as *Sid And Nancy*, which will appear later in our story.

And so a pattern emerged as the cast list was revealed. Temple and, to a lesser extent, McLaren clearly wanted to celebrate the tacky, insalubrious end of British culture as much as knock the Pistols off their pedestal. Elsewhere they brought in an array of faded ex-stars from the end-of-the-pier area of Britain's domestic film industry: the role of cinema usherette was played by Irene Handl, who had defined a series of thick-skinned roles as landladies, mothers-in-law and so on since the previous decade.

Jess Conrad was another actor whose star had faded. A middle-aged theater, film and TV 'face', his career included a series of pop singles for the Decca label in the late 1950s and early 1960s (he was voted Most Popular Singer in 1961 in *NME*'s annual poll). Stints as Jesus in *Godspell* and Joseph in *Joseph And The Amazing Technicolor Dreamcoat* revived his career and he remained a popular draw until the 1980s, when he moved to the *Crossroads* soap opera and other undemanding TV fare.

It wasn't all washed-up light-entertainment actors, however. The best-known female punk, Pamela 'Jordan' Rooke, made a cameo appearance wearing a T-shirt sporting the words 'Only Anarchists Are Pretty.' After her stint as a model for Vivienne Westwood's punk fashion designs, Jordan had gained some notoriety when Lydon stripped her clothes off on-stage at an early Pistols gig. Far from being a punk stooge, however, she went on to manage Adam & The Ants— then very much a punk band. She also appeared in what would be hailed as the only other punk film of substance, 1977's *Jubilee*, directed by Derek Jarman. In the early 1980s, Jordan stepped out of public view and moved to the south coast, where she worked as a veterinary nurse and bred Burmese cats. "Punk, really, died for me when the Pistols split up," she said. "It couldn't have gone on. It was like an orgasm—there were a few seconds then... pfft."

Meanwhile, behind the scenes, Don Boyd and Jeremy Thomas oversaw the project as executive producers for Kendon Films, ostensibly the production company alongside McLaren's Matrixbest outfit. Distribution was agreed with Virgin, who were in the process of releasing the Pistols' first (and only) LP at the time of negotiations.

The soundtrack, co-ordinated by Andy Walker, was also to be released by Virgin as a standalone album to accompany the film; it became the only other official album release by the Pistols at the time. Lydon's absence was got round by having Jones and Cook re-record guitar and drum parts to a set of demos from October 1976, which already had Lydon's vocals on them. In this way a relatively fresh set of songs was created for the movie, although—perhaps in the spirit of McLaren's quasi-nihilistic attitude towards his band and their fans, the buyers were in many cases getting rehashed versions of product which they already had.

Finally, the animated sections were handled by Derek W. Hayes, Bill Mather and others, and the task of editing the many hundreds of film snippets into a coherent whole was taken on by a team including Richard Bedford, Crispin Green, Mike Maslin, Bernie Pokrzywa and David Rae.

Once the laborious task of editing the finished footage was underway in autumn 1978, and the band members had gone their separate ways, a release point could be put on *The Great Rock 'n' Roll Swindle*. A date sometime in mid-1979 was mooted and a tentative schedule correspondingly arranged.

By this stage, however, the relationship between McLaren and Temple had soured and progress was delayed. As Temple told Rob Hughes at *Record Collector*, "At the end... Malcolm was trying to fire me and there was all sorts going on. But I was determined not to be fired, because I'd put three years into the film."

The breakdown in the relationship was not an unexpected development in anyone's eyes. As the director explained, the manager became frustrated during the long editing process— which took place in a small studio above a laundrette in Soho with snow coming in from the ceiling—and demanded that the 'middle-class bastard' Temple be 'a slave' (his actual words, according to the director) in the process, without even being permitted to talk. Needless to say this was unacceptable to Temple, and McLaren stormed off, taking his name off the film and leaving Temple to finish the edit and submit it for manufacture.

In late 1978 the spotlight shifted to the tragic figure of Sid Vicious, who had careered from crisis to crisis in the wake of the Pistols' split. Battling his heroin and methadone dependency with frequent lapses, accompanied by the equally erratic Nancy Spungen, Vicious—far from preparing for solo stardom—was spiralling into chaos.

Having settled in New York in August 1978, the couple made a local name for themselves with alacrity, just as they had when living in London's Maida Vale. (One Spungen story from the London era told that Vicious had once locked her out of their flat; her response was to run up and down the street, dressed only in a G-string, shouting "I love you.") Holed up in a $30-per-night room at the notorious Chelsea Hotel on 23rd Street—the former hangout of luminaries such as Bob Dylan, Patti Smith and The Grateful Dead—with only a kitten for company, Vicious and Spungen would spend days in a haze of heroin, paid for from bags of money which Nancy would carry around with her as the couple's finance manager.

The first bombshell came in 13 October, when the news broke that Vicious had been arrested in Room 100 at the Chelsea for the murder of Spungen. She had died from a deep abdominal stab wound at some point the previous night. As reported in the *New York Post*, Vicious had been out of sorts for some time previously—one unnamed associate stated that Spungen had "begged him to go home with them because Vicious was acting strange and had pressed his hunting knife against her throat a few days earlier." "He beat her with a guitar every so often but I didn't think he was going to kill her," said the same source.

"There was a violent episode four days before she died," wrote Spungen's mother Deborah later on. "She said he'd been hitting her. I spent the next days worrying. And then she didn't call. And never called again."

Perhaps this turn of events was inevitable. "There was one incident which has left a lasting impression, but infer from it what you will," Don Letts once recalled. "I remember I went out to New York. I had to get Sid's signature for his appearances in *The Punk Rock Movie*. He sat on a sofa, playing with Nancy. He had this huge six-inch blade knife, and he just kept on prodding her with it. A week later she was dead."

The police reported that there were signs of a struggle in the room and a trail of blood leading to the bathroom, where Spungen, wearing black underwear and covered in blood, was found. As Vicious, pale and dazed, was led away, he threatened to "smash the cameras" of the waiting press.

The couple's lifestyle had been famously erratic—both had often stated they would die young, and Nancy once said: "I'll kill myself as soon as the first wrinkle appears"—so few observers were surprised that such an incident had occurred. Most, however, were shocked at the idea of Sid committing such a violent crime. Hotel staff reported that their switchboard had received an outside call urging them to check Room 100—because "someone is seriously injured and I'm not kidding, man"—and a bellman subsequently investigated.

Vicious wasn't there when the employee entered the room and found the body, but reappeared shortly after.

"We get a very creative mix," hotel manager Stanley Bard said as Vicious was removed. "Every once in a while you get a music group that is crazy."

Vicious' story was slightly different, and went that he had awoken late at night and had seen Nancy with a hunting knife that they had bought earlier that day. He then awoke at 11.15am after taking the depressant Tuinal, discovered that Nancy was not in bed with him and then found her body in the bathroom. He then called reception and asked for an ambulance, which arrived accompanied by police, who arrested Vicious, detained him at the East 51st Street station and charged him with the murder at 5:30pm that afternoon.

As with so many rock 'n' roll death trips, confusion and paranoia about the event circulated, fuelled partly by later articles in *Rolling Stone*, whose writer Michael Segell put in some impressive investigative work. Apparently Spungen had just received a cheque from Malcolm McLaren, as well as $3,000 from various public appearances Vicious had made. She then ordered some Dilaudid (synthetic morphine) from a friend called Rockets Redglare, who stayed with them until about 5am on the day of the arrest. On leaving, Redglare saw another drug supplier in the hotel reception, heading for the lift.

Another story revealed that Neon Leon, a musician who also lived in the Chelsea Hotel, had Sex Pistols clippings, Sid's leather jacket and gold records in his room. Leon claimed that the couple knocked on his door at 3am and left the items with him.

A third, unproven, theory goes that Spungen was murdered by a drug dealer while Vicious was high and unconscious—for refusing to return some of the drugs they had bought from him earlier that day. The dealer could have used Vicious's knife, wearing gloves to avoid fingerprints and leaving Sid's earlier prints on it.

Support for Vicious came from his old friend John Lydon in a *Melody Maker* feature the week after his arrest. In it the former Pistols singer declared: "Sid isn't capable of killing her. It's not possible… No, it is *not* possible. Full stop. It sounds so corny when you say 'a victim of circumstance'. I won't comment—I don't want to be printed as saying anything about it. God, it's so difficult. Say it was a close friend of yours and the press wanted a comment because it's good press. You feel so bad. I don't want to know—I just want to keep out. Malcolm's making a lot of money out of Sid's personal tragedy, and that offends me. There's not too much I can do about it either. It's as simple as that."

Drugs had turned Vicious away from Lydon, the latter explained. Vicious had started using heroin "as soon he had money. Before that it was just speed and silly things that don't make much difference to your life anyway. But then he was impressed by this groupie from New York—like most silly arseholes he had this delusion about New York being the hip place, man, where it all happens, and it doesn't: it's a shithole, it's just one big Dingwalls… You see, Sid decided quite some time ago that he was going to become an arsehole, and he did."

Heroin had not impressed the perceptive Lydon. "All that fucking heroin shit, it just got on my nerves. I mean, yeah, people take it once in a while, but not every fucking day.

And then that decadence trip that he got into—you know, cutting himself and ugh! It's nothing... It was boring, it was fucking silly. He couldn't play the bass and it made doing gigs just a waste of time 'cos I had no idea what was going on behind me. There was no tune that I could pick out on—one song sounded very much like any other one. It just all became pointless."

Lydon reserved some bile for his former manager McLaren, adding: "I'm sure Malcolm's looking after his best interests... he's going to make a wonderful film out of it... He'll try and make a bigger cunt out of Sid than he is already. So I have no comment, 'cos nothing I can say or do will change that situation... Sid to me is a mate. He's always been a dodo. I've known him a long while, but I won't comment on that kind of scandal... He's been manipulated—that is the problem. Most people are just accepting that he did it, and Malcolm is doing nothing to solve that."

McLaren had, on the face of it, looked after his client to a degree. After Vicious was charged with second degree murder, bail was set at $50,000. *The Sun* wrote of the trial, "Sex Pistol Sid Vicious almost collapsed in court yesterday when he was accused of murdering his blonde girlfriend Nancy Spungen. The 21-year-old spiky-haired punk star seemed to be in a trance as he was led into the New York court by a detective. Before his appearance, Vicious denied killing Nancy, a 20-year-old American go-go dancer...

"In court, Vicious was helped to a chair as he staggered and buckled at the knees. His body shuddered periodically as he spent the rest of the 10-minute hearing with his head resting on a table. Throughout, he seemed oblivious to the proceedings as he was formally charged with murder under his real name, John Simon Ritchie. If convicted, he faces a prison sentence of 20 years to life."

Vicious was then removed to Riker's Island prison and settled into the hospital wing to undergo heroin detoxification.

After hiring the firm of Pryor, Cashman, Sherman and Flynn to defend him, McLaren arranged for Virgin Records to put up Vicious' bail. "Malcolm wouldn't even put up the bail himself," Lydon said. "The record companies had to do it—that's how great Malcolm is. And then he goes to the press saying 'I'm doing everything I can to help Sid' when all he's doing is making a film… Let's face it, if Sid gets fucking life that's a perfect ending for Malcolm's *Rock 'n' Roll Swindle.*"

When the money arrived on 16 October, McLaren went to Riker's Island and took the paroled Vicious to the Hotel Seville on Madison Avenue. There they were joined by Vicious' mother Ann Beverly, who had financed her trip to the US by raising $10,000 from the sale of her inside story to the *New York Post*.

Things went from bad to much worse. Depressed by his girlfriend's death and in terrible anguish about his possible part in it, Vicious attempted suicide on 22 October by slashing his wrists and overdosing on methadone, the heroin substitute he'd been prescribed as part of his rehab.

After rushing Vicious to hospital, McLaren told *Melody Maker*: "He had been suffering rapid methadone withdrawal over the weekend, and by that evening he panicked. Sid is all right now—they patched up his arms and gave him 50 milligrammes of methadone, which has stabilized him. He was anxious to get himself clear of drugs, and was trying to come off it too quickly. It's impossible for anyone who hasn't been through that to know what it means."

The manager added that short-term plans—if Vicious was willing—included the possible recording of an album or some filming, for two reasons. Firstly, Sid's trial for Nancy's murder would require him to be in as healthy as state as possible. "I wanted him fit mentally and physically for the ordeal of the trial, and I felt he would need an objective to steer himself away from all the problems that will constantly nag at him until the trial is over. That's why I suggested some recording to him."

Secondly, the costs of the defence team—estimated by some at over $100,000, a vast sum in 1978—would require funds: "Also the enormous costs of getting the strongest defence lawyer I can find will provide us with considerable financial problems, which a record will help solve."

Asked if he had been filming the current events in New York to use in the *Swindle*, he said no—but added that if Vicious was interested, filming might take place later.

After a recovery in November, and the acquisition of a new girlfriend named Michelle Robinson, Vicious was seen out and about once more on the New York scene. But trouble lay around the corner. On 9 December he was involved in a fight with Patti Smith's brother Todd at a club called Hurrah's. Smith punched him and Vicious replied with a broken bottle, cutting Smith's face. Police arrested Vicious and—as he had violated the terms of his parole—took him back into custody at Riker's Island.

Over almost seven weeks, Vicious cleaned up completely and he was released on 1 February 1979. With terrible irony, his release would be the death of him. He left Riker's at noon, went to a friend's apartment in Greenwich Village to celebrate his release, and immediately injected some heroin—bought for him by his mother Ann Beverly. With his system newly healed, he didn't enjoy the hit fully, and asked for more. His mother obliged. After a few minutes Vicious collapsed on a bed. His friends wondered if they should take him to a hospital but he denied that he had overdosed.

In the early hours of the morning of 2 February, Vicious woke up, found a lethal amount of heroin in his mother's purse, used it—and died.

The following day, *The Daily Mail* said: "Punk rock star Sid Vicious, the inadequate youth who turned a tasteless pop gimmick into pathetic real life, died of a heroin overdose yesterday. His body was found after a party in his new girlfriend's apartment in Greenwich Village, New York, held to celebrate his release from jail on bail."

Later, Ann Beverly wrote: "I swear to God he appeared to have a pink aura around his whole body... he was lying there quite peacefully. I shook him until I realised he was very cold and very dead."

Beverly's view was that he had overdosed deliberately, offering as evidence a piece of paper on which he had written: "You were my little baby girl / And I knew all your fears / Such joy to hold you in my arms / And kiss away your tears / But now you're gone / There's only pain / And nothing I can do / And I don't want to live this life / If I can't live for you."

And so the scene was set. "It was a nightmare!" said Temple. Sid and Nancy were dead, Lydon was off with his new band

and the Pistols' legacy was smoking in the dust. Who knew if there would even be an audience for the movie, when it finally appeared? No one could have foreseen what final form the movie would take when it was at last released in October 1979. Temple and McLaren had created a monster.

kill your idols: scene by scene

"If your civilisation produces Nazis,
then that civilisation is rubbish"

Vivienne Westwood

Taking his cue partly from heroes such as the French director Jean-Luc Godard—whose innovative, political, directorial style had impressed him as a film student—and partly out of sheer necessity due to the number of unrelated snippets of film he had to use, Julien Temple structured the film in ten chapters. Each was headed by a 'lesson' from Malcolm McLaren on how to—and how dated this sounds today—"make a million pounds" from the record industry.

In doing so, Temple made McLaren—a manager, whose place is usually in the background—effectively the main character and central narrator of the whole film. Although this may sound like an exercise in vanity on McLaren's part—and there is an undeniable plausibility to that—the device works, largely because it links up the chaotic tale of the Pistols and divides it into a series of episodic chunks that are easy to digest. It also highlights key events by making them signposts for each of McLaren's lessons. The reasoning seems to have been that even if the audience didn't like the film, its message and its content would be simpler to understand, and thus the job of de-idolizing the Pistols would be achieved.

It's a sinister beginning, all right. As the words 'Boyd's Co. and Virgin Films present…' appear on screen, a gimp mask—an S&M mask made of rubber or plastic like a balaclava with eye holes—dominates the screen, with two eyes peering out. The mask has an inflatable section, designed to cause maximum pain and thus humiliation to the wearer, who in this case is Malcolm McLaren, whose nickname 'The Embezzler' appears in the credits. With a satanic whisper, McLaren delivers a monologue, the contents of which are only half-intelligible.

The serious tone doesn't last. Temple breaks down the mood by jumping to a mock-up of the Gordon Riots, the anti-Catholic mob violence of 1780 London. Dressed in fake Regency garb and resembling nothing more than a pack of failed Adam & The Ants auditionees, various student-actor types run through the streets and some darkened fields, yelling and waving in celebration. A bonfire rages and a gibbet looms high in the sky. Effigies—somewhere between blow-up sex dolls and Guy Fawkes dummies—are tossed from person to person. On examination they're clearly supposed to represent the Sex Pistols, although only the Rotten version is really recognizable. With shouts of glee and rather forced 'anarchic' revelry, the crowd half-burns them on the bonfire before stringing them up to be hanged. The four figures are suspended, revolving mournfully, as Temple's pack of student extras mill around below them.

It's a laughable scene which seems to have been created by film-school undergraduates with no budget and a dressing-up box left over from a sixth-form *King Lear*, but it performs its function—an allegory of the persecution of the Pistols, with literal 'anarchy' implications. In fact, its homemade feel provides much of its charm: the punk movement was, after all, the first to tell people *en masse* that a DIY approach to music, business and life itself was the way forward. And it's redeemed by the remarkable soundtrack, a string orchestra's version of 'God Save The Queen,' wailing violins copying the "No future..." melody and all.

Interspersed with the riot scenes are shots of Malcolm McLaren at home, seated at a table and instructing his assistant, the dwarf Helen Wellington-Lloyd (aka Helen of Troy), to burn various Pistols memorabilia—posters, magazines, the sleeve of *Never Mind The Bollocks... Here's The Sex Pistols*—on an open fire. The flames consume the products and burn fiercely, with a close-up on record labels and logos of Virgin and others.

Lesson One: How To Manufacture Your Group
McLaren and Helen are seen leaving the building—actually the former's Sex shop at 430 King's Road—and walking out into the street. The manager is in full S&M wear, with his bondage headgear giving him a strange, alien, look. He speaks to his assistant with a lilting accent, perhaps an imitation of Yiddish. As Temple remarked, "I think there is a bit of Fagin going on here."

The next scene is key to the whole film. Far from telling the Pistols' story in a chronological manner, Temple takes a film crew to the auditions for Lydon's replacement. While Vicious, Cook and Jones mime to a backing track in a rehearsal room, a series of young men—all comparing badly to the departed Lydon—bawl out lyrics of their own creation and attempt appropriately punkish stage moves. One of them is much more impressive than the rest. This is Edward Tudor-Pole, a gaunt, pale, man with a shock of dark hair whose spastic, eminently watchable, act is his own and no one else's.

Tudor-Pole claims to be a direct descendant of Henry VIII, hence the Tudor part of his name. "The Pole bit goes back hundreds of years, to the Norman Conquest. I'm really Edward Pole but my great-grandfather did some genealogy and worked out some connection with the royal house of Tudor, so he added Tudor to the Pole. So it's a bit bogus really—you can blame my grandfather!" He had impressed Temple by flipping a cigarette end off the floor with the broken flap of the sole of his shoe and catching it in his mouth, although it is not known if he was seriously considered for the position of singer based on such tricks.

Tudor-Pole's musical experience was limited, but he had been in a band called The Visitors. "I'd just left drama school and the punk thing was just erupting," he said. "I answered an advert in the *Melody Maker*, which said 'Wild front man wanted.' I thought, 'That's me!' I got the job, we did a few gigs and got a few fans... We did some demos, but the songs weren't very good. I was just the singer: I didn't do anything creative for them. We played at the Marquee and got a review, which said 'the band are excellent apart from the bug-eyed cretin on vocals'! So they sacked me, basically."

A few weeks later one of his ex-bandmates told him that the Pistols were looking for a new singer. "If he hadn't phoned me up I wouldn't have known about it and wouldn't have gone along," mused Tudor-Pole. "So I just went along to the audition for the *Rock 'n' Roll Swindle...*"

As Julien Temple was auditioning the bulk of the candidates on the first day, Tudor-Pole knew he had to make an impression. "This was the first day, the opening gambit. I'd been at drama school and the audition was in a theatre. All the other lads [had] piled in the front and were sitting around in the stalls waiting their turn: a man with a clipboard was saying 'What's your name, who's next?' So I went in at the stage door, found my way to the stage and made a massive entrance! If you're on stage you've got the attention of the entire theatre… I walked onto that stage and commanded the room, and said 'Hello, I'm Ten Tudor-Pole, are these the auditions for *Hamlet*?' and they all laughed. It's on your first entrance you're made. It's been the same ever since.

The auditions took the form of performing to a pre-recorded backing track. As Tudor-Pole recalled, "When we turned up, they gave us all a cassette to listen to a recording of the song with just Steve singing it. We had to learn it—we all had a sheet with the words on it. They gave us an hour or two to swot up on it, before we actually did it on stage.

"They whittled it down to the final four or something, to do it the next day with the Pistols. The Pistols were miming, with each of us doing a version of the 'Great Rock 'n' Roll Swindle' track, and they spliced it up. The audition is as seen in the film, but all cut together."

The Sex Pistols were not present on that first day but Sid Vicious and Nancy Spungen were, and typically Vicious made a spectacle of himself.

"Sid came in with Nancy and we were all thinking, 'Fuck, that's Sid Vicious!' Nancy was really loudly obnoxious and Sid's slumped in a stall seat. She got on stage and did a mock striptease, got down to her bra and pants and said, 'I'm not taking any more off, the rest is reserved for Siddy boy.' She wasn't being amusing about it.

"Then suddenly Sid turned round—he was near the front of the stalls and a lot of us were at the back. He turned around, he was obviously out of it, and said, 'Why don't you lot all fuck off?' One of the people sitting behind me who was auditioning as well, said 'Bollocks!' Sid lost his temper! 'You said "Bollocks" to me!' He jumped out of his seat, came running up to the back of the theatre and started punching the bloke. This bloke was trying to fend him off as he was being hit by his hero! He was saying, 'Sid man, cool it!' It soon settled down and they were sitting next to each other chatting."

Although these were genuine auditions, the search for a singer for the Sex Pistols—a dying band with internal tensions tearing it apart and no real future—can only have been staged for the cameras. The film-makers had advertised for a singer without telling the applicants that the process was to be included in a movie, and the auditions were to provide an opportunity for them to show what they thought a Pistols singer should look like, with public embarrassment and derision the inevitable outcome.

This kind of *Schadenfreude*—enjoyment of others' misfortunes—informs the entire length of *The Great Rock 'n' Roll Swindle*, right to its very core. Despite its entertaining façade as a light-hearted caper in which the Pistols and McLaren rob the rich (the record companies) and give to the poor (or at least show them how to do it too), the *Swindle* is at heart a callous film. We all delight in the downfall of institutions at times: it's human nature to do so. But the movie is a long, harsh, celebration of nihilism—of the joy in fleecing people, of the acquisition of money for its own sake, of encouraging failure and depression and cheapness.

In this it's a microcosm of later punk. Punk had begun life as an ideal based on a fiery optimism—do it yourself; smash the system; three chords and the truth—but it had declined into a state of disillusioned torpor. We could say that the story of punk is the story of the Sex Pistols; we could add that the story of *The Great Rock 'n' Roll Swindle* is the story of punk. But in the fictional world on screen—and fiction it is, even if the events are real—we're shown the dark underbelly of late-1970s culture.

And so the boys who audition are mocked—and we mock right along with them. Temple added that while he was in Brazil, word got around that Rio's rumored resident Nazi, Martin Bormann, was to join the band as Lydon's replacement. Now *that* would have made McLaren smile…

The scene ends with Helen of Troy finishing the assembly of the film's title from large foam blocks. Rolling around like a child, she adds a human full stop to the punkish text.

Immediately we're reminded of the iconic work done for the Pistols by their associate Jamie Reid, whose graphic approach was such a crucial part of their image. As he told *Index* magazine, he and McLaren had known each other as students protesting against the authorities at the college they attended. "In the early 1970s, myself and a group of friends formed a collective to start a community printing press… which was producing quick and fast leaflets, pamphlets, books, anarchist cookbooks, things for the women's movement, the black movement, squatting.

"In terms of graphic design, I probably learned more from the printing press than I did in art school. You start developing an appreciation for what actually looks good—out of sheer necessity, from having no money. Some things gain qualities, some things lose qualities. We had to produce things really fast... In very many ways, that was the look that later became associated with the Pistols and punk. Its whole base was anarchist community situations and the printing press. And then just moving it into popular culture, which was quite a conscious thing on my and Malcolm's parts. That's what we did."

He went on: "The whole Situationist, anarchistic element that's within all that—it's like a re-evaluation of history which, to a big extent, is what the 1990s is very much about. From the Surrealists and the Dadaists to the Situationists and the whole movement of community agit-prop politics, down into punk and then into all sorts of things... the move into the punk thing was a sort of disillusionment with the whole over-intellectualisation of what happened with the Situationist movement and the politics of the 1970s. It was an attempt to take those movements into popular culture."

Even as early as 1969 and 1970, taking the movements into popular culture had included printing subversive posters with slogans such as 'Keep Warm This Winter— Make Trouble' and 'Save Petrol—Burn Cars' and sticking the word 'Lies' over advertisements. "There was all sorts of stuff," the artist recalled. "It was a whole group of us in London [but] you've got to remember that there were community presses all over Britain. People were out doing stuff, sending stuff to each other. Pranksterism was very much a big part of the whole thing, a lot of humor as well... we got away with murder. And it's still something that's continued. It hasn't gone away."

Reid's reunion with his college friend McLaren came in the early 1970s.

"I'd kept in contact with Malcolm, and one day got a telegram saying, 'Come down, we've got this project in London we want you to work on'—which happened to be the Sex Pistols... I got a job at a printing press in south London, which was actually a Labour Party printing press. That's where we were doing all the early Pistols stuff. We just went for it. It was like that for four years—an enormous amount of spontaneity. And it was a much more collective situation than probably Malcolm or John Lydon are willing to acknowledge. It was sort of fan-based, about 50 people who were very much as important a part of it as the band were."

Once he began work on the Pistols' material, Reid rapidly brought an identity to it that was absolutely key. As he told *Eyestorm*, "I am a great admirer of Jackson Pollock's work, though this influence can probably be most easily seen on my painted works. The work I did for the Pistols was, to a large extent, more 'graphic,' though I tend not to differentiate and am happy to fuse whatever elements are most relevant at the time...

"In the context of the Pistols, the 'I'm A Mess' image of Sid Vicious was probably the most 'painterly' I got. This image, photographed by Bob Gruen, was used as a promotional poster for the 'Something Else' single in 1979. Kurt Schwitters' collage works were definitely something I looked at, and was fully aware of from art school days; a pioneer and master of 'cut and paste'. Man Ray: again, [I was] aware of his works, though I can't really say that they had any direct influence on my Pistols works. Dada, John Heartfield, George

Grosz, Raoul Hausmann, though not directly, did have more of an influence on these works, more so than Man Ray."

Lesson Two: Establish The Name Sex Pistols

'Never mind the bollocks' went the slogan, and to emphasize to the point Malcolm McLaren's own testicles are seen in a bathtub as he tells Helen his second lesson. Reclining amid a bubble-bath, the manager looks on as she walks across the room writes some text on the stomach of a naked, barely pubescent girl who stands against a wall. A montage of shots sees the girl evolve from an innocent child to the well-known punkette Sue 'Catwoman' Lucas, a Pistols associate whose trademark blonde/brunette 'ears' haircut and eye make-up provided her nickname.

Temple later recalled that the film-makers had almost got into trouble by using the young girl in the scene, not because of her nakedness—which would have outraged many viewers today—but because they cut her hair, a liberty which her guardians had not expected or agreed to. However, she was widely thought to be underage at the time of filming—and on the VHS or later DVD version of the *Swindle*, sharp-eyed viewers will notice a fake pair of panties which have been dubbed on to hide her nakedness.

As McLaren speaks, his head moves nervously from side to side, as if he's searching for something. This lends him a slightly unhinged, dictatorial, air, although in fact he was just looking for the cards pinned up around the set which bore his lines. "Malcolm's never been the easiest person to get along with," said Temple. "All the words he speaks in the film were on little filing cards. So when you see him staring around the room, he's really looking for those. It added a certain dementia to the proceedings. He took the whole project seriously enough to be able to make fun of it, though."

We then move to a nightclub scene via an in-car shot depicting Boogie, the Pistols' tour manager, as chauffeur of the band's limousine. (According to Temple, Boogie did an invaluable job of keeping the four Pistols together on the road, getting them out of bed on time and to the venue without delay. He was perhaps the most professional non-musical associate of the entire organisation.) The club scene, as is revealed later on, is a clever montage of the Pistols live on TV, filmed directly from a television set—intercut with crowd scenes from an actual club. The dancers are an eye-opening sight at three decades' distance. The early punk crowds, with white face-paint giving them a ghoulish look more associated with today's black metal movement rather than the punk scene, grab each other's heads and shake them violently as part of their dancing.

Meanwhile the band, whose sepia-toned performance makes it clear that they're not actually in front of the full-color crowd, are giving a visceral, vitriolic performance. Original bassist Glen Matlock appears stage left, showing a grasp of bass-playing never equalled by Sid Vicious—but none of the latter's twisted, nihilistic arrogance either. Such snippets of film had been recorded by Temple and stored for just this opportunity. When the time came to cut the fragments together, he relished the chance to employ a cut-and-paste technique. Here, it works perfectly. The Pistols in the live arena never looked so good or so aggressive.

The nightclub scene is followed by the first scene of a subplot in which Steve Jones, dressed in the trenchcoat and hat of a clichéd 1950s film-noir private detective—complete with first-person narrative, is introduced. On the hunt for McLaren for reasons that are never revealed but seem to involve some deep-seated need for revenge (Jones is cast as The Crook), he pads the streets of London, taking in its most insalubrious locations. He breaks into the Glitterbest offices—this scene was filmed in McLaren's real-life office—and opens the safe. Nothing of interest is found so he plans his next move.

Jones' performance throughout the film is surprisingly assured. Although he isn't a trained actor, the natural confidence and gobby arrogance that took him from petty crime to threatening audiences worldwide carries him through. This was the result of Temple's restrained directing presence. A young man himself, he brought out the best in the youthful Pistol by allowing his natural personality to come through, flaws and all.

Lesson Three: Sell The Swindle
The next footage comes from director Derek Jarman, who filmed The Pistols in 1975 at a warehouse party. The grainy, hand-held, Super 8 film reveals a young band who are far from being the sloppy amateurs we had been led to expect. Matlock, Jones and Cook power through a surprisingly solid version of 'Johnny B Goode' while the incredibly young-looking Lydon mugs his way through the lyrics—or at least those that he knows. Most of the time he bellows a series of la-la-la's.

The venue was the private residence of the sculptor and socialite Andrew Logan at Butler's Wharf, Tower Bridge. The stage on which the band performed was the set from the court scene in Jarman's film *Sebastiane*, with a toy castle that Logan had bought at the recently closed Biba's store. Pamela 'Jordan' Rooke stripped to the waist on stage, and Chrissie Hynde (later of The Pretenders, at this point one of the Bromley Contingent of Pistols followers) was also at the party.

The Bromley Contingent—as they were labelled by a clever journalist at the *NME*—were, it seems, encouraged to form by McLaren so a scene would appear to coalesce around the Pistols. They included the aforementioned Sue 'Catwoman' Lucas, Simon Barker, Debbie 'Juvenile' Wilson (later a model for softcore magazines such as *Men Only*), Linda Ashby, Philip Salon and Bertie 'Berlin' Marshall, who worked as a male prostitute and later became an author. Some of the Contingent—including William 'Billy Idol' Broad, Siouxsie Sioux and Steve Severin—went on to be musicians too, either as part of the punk movement or in the later New Romantic scene.

Of the so-called Bromley Contingent, future Ant Marco Pirroni explained: "I think it was a collection of people like me, really. In Bromley [in suburban Kent] there was four or five of them. Just individuals who turned their mate onto it, their only friend who would listen to the Velvet Underground. So it was more than eight people, but none of them were connected in any way.

"The [Sex] shop was the connection when people came together, and obviously [there was a] visual thing, which was really important. You're walking down the King's Road, and you saw somebody else coming towards you and you think, 'They're alright, they've got Sex stuff on.' But of course you didn't speak!... Too cool to do that! The idea was of the boutique, which people don't do any more. Individual shops doing individual clothes that you can only buy at that shop. So if you wanted those clothes, you had to go to that shop. So you could be a fan of that shop, and you could dress in that scene, and be part of the scene, part of the set."

Vivienne Westwood made quite an impression on Pirroni. "When I saw Vivienne," he recalled, "I thought 'I've never seen anyone who looks like this in my entire life.' I was a bit shell-shocked because I went into this shop and it wasn't like anything else. It felt like it had a history—it felt funky and sexy and dangerous. It was a bit scary. She was nice, but she was slightly scary. It was perfectly fine, but you think, 'Where does she go? What does she do?' I was 13—she must have been about 28 or 29. She looked like no one I'd ever seen, but looked amazing. You look at her, and you think 'I want to be like that.'"

Once a scene had developed around the shop, there was no turning back. "If you go in once a week, people start saying hello," said Pirroni. "I started thinking, 'I want to have something in common with these people.' Malcolm was the chatty one, we could talk... Vivienne is slightly mad—only *slightly*... she's certainly madder than Malcolm. I can understand where Malcolm's coming from, why he does things. Vivienne I just don't. Sitting there in the shop and talking to Malcolm, made me realize things. He'd say, 'What do you do?' I'd say, 'Well, I go to school, I go to Harrow Uxbridge.' He'd say, 'Oh, I went there—you won't learn nothing there.' And that stuck with me. I thought, 'I'm not fucking learning anything. What *am* I doing there?'"

Back in the movie, the action shifts to Highgate Village, the elaborate private houses near the famous cemetery in north London. It's Jones the private detective again, stalking McLaren but finding only a plummy-voiced singing coach named Tona de Brett, who had once tried to train John Lydon's voice. Jones peers through a window (intercut to give the impression that he is there at the time of de Brett's interview, which was actually an earlier piece of footage) and prefaces her self-introduction with the snarled question, "Who the fuck are you?"

De Brett tells the story of Lydon's lesson, and it's not pretty. According to her, he would start a song in one key and restart it in another when she tried to accompany him. It must have been a major ego boost for McLaren to hear her add that, perversely, "Lydon's manager had a beautiful ear" as he went on to launch a short-lived career himself in the mid-1980s.

"I've seen the bit of the film with me in it," comments de Brett, "although that was quite some time ago. I didn't really expect to be in the film, as I didn't take any of it at all seriously. Also, they only paid me a pittance!"

She's under no illusions as to why Temple included her in such an anti-establishment movie. "I think they included me because they thought it would be a giggle to include a posh, middle-aged singing teacher in amongst all the punks!"

The idea of the relentlessly 'we mean it man' Lydon visiting a singing teacher is a snare cast by McLaren to fool shallower viewers into considering the Pistols frontman a fake. While it's true that the punk scene sought to denounce the vanities of the mainstream rock that had preceded it—and singing lessons might be included among these—there's nothing remotely anti-punk about Lydon seeking to strengthen his style with professional help. What makes it entertaining is the juxtaposition of Lydon and de Brett, an upper-class, highly educated woman who spoke like the Queen. The inclusion of the scene is an invaluable insight into McLaren's motives when writing and assembling the film—and his attitude to his former protégé Lydon.

Shifting to the nearby cemetery and the dead of night, we next see McLaren and Helen enact an almost Shakespearean piece of vaudeville (at one point Helen leaps into Malcolm's arms). Singing the old Max Bygraves song 'You Need Hands' while carrying a sputtering torch and dressed in a tartan suit and 'Cash From Chaos' T-shirt, McLaren and his assistant—who utters not a word throughout the entire *Swindle*—stick posters to the walls of the old cemetery buildings. It's an act of near-desecration aimed directly at the establishment via the old walls of tradition. Above one of the arches from which they emerge is a cobbled-together coat of arms bearing a scrawled 'MM' at its centre and the logos of EMI, A&M and Virgin—an amusing bit of vanity.

Lesson Four: Don't Play, Don't Give The Game Away

A truck driver sits eating his dinner in front of the TV. The screen bears the words 'Censored by Thames TV', but we can hear the soundtrack. It's the Bill Grundy show, and Steve Jones' cackling retorts of "You dirty old fucker!" and "You fucking rotter!" are heard. The burly fellow leaps up in anger and puts his foot through the TV screen, a reaction made famous by the subsequent tabloid coverage.

Ironically, the Grundy incident is said to have visibly shaken McLaren, who hustled his band into a limo after the show and away from the scene as rapidly as possible, swearing that their behavior on prime-time TV had undone all his hard work. If true, this was an unusual, eye-off-the-ball moment for the manager. Famously on the pulse when it came to organizing off-the-shelf controversy, he might be expected to have planned or the whole event. But it seems he too was experiencing a steep learning curve when it came to the Pistols.

The publicity, of course, was priceless. A week of red-top frothing followed as the nation's papers squeezed every drop out of the event. However, one negative consequence was the refusal of many of the country's live venues to allow the band to perform there, leading to a situation in which the Pistols were travelling the country in a bus looking for places to play. As the 'lesson' for this episode, 'Don't Play, Don't Earn Money' might have seemed equally apposite.

McLaren and his secretary Sophie Richmond—the girlfriend of Pistols designer Jamie Reid and, according to Temple, the real organizational brains behind the band's everyday activities—are then seen in the Glitterbest offices, mulling over the situation. This modern, urban scene contrasts starkly with the next one, a night-time shoot (on 14 December 1976) in Caerphilly in Glamorgan.

Outside the town's Castle Cinema a group of local churchgoers are seen braving the winter cold to sing hymns and generally express their disapproval of the Sex Pistols gig there. A stand-off between band (indoors, safely out of the cold—Lydon expresses sarcastic acknowledgement of the fact) and locals is unresolved, the only real point of interest being the explanations of their actions by a couple of the pious protesters.

Lesson Five: Steal Money From The Record Company Of Your Choice

Paul Cook lies in the cot of a baby's bedroom, which is decked out in Christmas decorations. He sleeps uneasily, dressed in the outfit of a Santa gnome. 'Watcha Gonna Do About It?' plays in the background as he twitches and turns. A satanic Santa, Steve Jones in appropriate attire, peers through the window at him.

The first of the animated episodes of the film then begins. Cartoonish and relentlessly unsophisticated, even by the standards of the day, these sections are perfect for depicting the Pistols' antics as they sign to EMI and celebrate in typical style. Records are flung across the office; Sid cuts himself and stumbles hurriedly through the gents' toilets, dripping blood and looking for a bandage; Jones is discovered having sex with an unidentified EMI employee; and the staff are generally horrified at the behavior of their latest signings. It's a cross between *Tom & Jerry*, *Carry On* and some darker, perhaps Situationist propaganda.

We next return to Steve Jones the detective, who enters a record company party with a cynical air. We still don't know why he's looking for Malcolm, but he takes a gold disc off the wall, pulls down his trousers and defecates on it. As he told one interviewer, "I know what it's like to squeeze one out," although he also admitted that the product in question was plastic.

Along the way he is engaged by a truculent record company executive, a woman with ants on her face. Some of these crawl slowly around her mouth and eyes as she lambasts Jones viciously as a "walking abortion" and a "walking dildo." This was a sideswipe at the feminist critics who had derided the Pistols as mere expressions of macho chauvinism with no real transcendence of their maleness: an opinion punctured by Temple's caricature. The words she uses are quotations from the notoriously vitriolic *SCUM Manifesto* by Valerie Solanas, published in 1967 as a call to arms against all men. (SCUM was an organisation of one; its initials stood for Society for Cutting Up Men.) Solanas later gained infamy by shooting her acquaintance Andy Warhol (he survived the attack) and died, a penniless prostitute, in 1988.

Temple's film-school pretentions are also visible in this scene: as he later commented, "You can get high on studying film." The ants on the vituperative woman's face are a homage of sorts to Luis Buñuel, the Mexican film-maker. His most controversial work, *Un Chien Andalou* (1929) is a short attack on bourgeois values and contains horrific scenes such as a woman's eyeball being slowly sliced open with a razor-blade and ants crawling from a hole in the centre of a man's hand. Temple knows his movie history and this scene is a public tribute. (Temple later encountered another invertebrate in Ultravox's 1981 video for their hit 'Vienna', in which he is pictured with a tarantula crawling across his face. "I was drunk," he confessed afterwards.)

You have to give the movie's creators credit: the next scene displays an impressive vision by showcasing the excellent, discofied funk of a band called The Black Arabs, whose deft versions of various Pistols tunes soundtrack a nightclub scene. McLaren walks into the club, telling the bouncer not to allow intruders in. The doorman, played by an uncredited Peter Dean (who would later find enduring, if unchallenging, small-screen success as stallholder Pete Beale in *EastEnders*) then refuses entry to an insistent Steve Jones, while McLaren guzzles beer from a balcony and watches the band play.

The idea of a black group incorporating punk music into their act is a concept that lies at the heart of the re-energized late-1970s music scene. As punk's first wave bloomed and spread from its white urban roots to the rest of society, among its earliest supporters were the dreads and Rastas who moved in the same circles. At its outset at least, punk was honest, emotional, music that didn't seek to impress (or trick) its listeners with intellectual artifice or elevated philosophy. It didn't need devices like this because it was fuelled by a different energy—anger. This anger came in turn from the injustices that its prime movers—Lydon especially—wrote about. Many of the black reggae, funk and soul fans of Britain lived in similarly poor circumstances, and so the message of punk resonated with them too.

We marvel at the dexterity of The Black Arabs, whose elaborately funky take on a clutch of Pistols standards gives them a swing and sexual drive that the original versions never had. Songs like 'Anarchy In The UK' were never about sex and soulfulness in their first incarnations: the raw, enraged shriek of Lydon and the trebly riffage of his band made those elements irrelevant. Funked up like this, the songs take on an entirely new timbre that some may dislike but all will find thought-provoking.

Lydon understood the pan-racial appeal of punk music, although he admitted that he'd found it a revelation at first. "Where was that gig where a lot of dreads turned up? That was really shocking. I think it was an early Nashville, years ago. There was a few of them at the back, and I was really shocked that they'd be there. I talked to them afterwards and they said, 'Understand, just understand, man will understand, mon.' You never get any trouble from blacks. They understand it's the same movement."

As the film-maker and DJ Don Letts told 3AM magazine, "I was a Brixton boy, born and bred. What you have to realize is that the blueprint for black people in Britain pre-Rasta was funk and soul... It was bullshit because it involved emulation of another culture, emulation of another host nation, while we as young black men should have been revelling in our differences, our qualities which were distinctly ours. So that's what Rasta and punk did for us, it freed us up! We didn't have to fall for the same 'cultural emulation' roles which our parents had succumbed to, which appeared to us as a form of cultural repression and castration...

"Also, there were new cultural exchanges going on among the black and white youth in London. I was hearing really freaky music like Captain Beefheart and Beatles tunes, and you know what? I loved that stuff. It wasn't like, 'Oh that's white man's shit!' I was being turned on by an alien culture, and essentially, this ongoing cultural exchange is what has inspired and informed me ever since. So out of this bad situation, good things were growing and it was a melting pot of influences going on! At the same time, all the hippest white guys were into checking out the latest funk clubs."

As for the moment when punk crossed over to Letts and other young black men of his generation, he explained: "Something really happened for me, and a lot of other people I came into contact with around this time. I have to say I learnt a lot from Vivienne and Malcolm. I learnt a lot regarding subversive elements in European culture. I learnt about the Situationists, like Guy Debord... which Malcolm and Vivienne were so into, but you have to realize they were truly fascinated by subversion in all its forms as it manifests itself in all cultures—and of course that involved understanding subversive undercurrents in Jamaican culture too. And that element was Rasta! So they learned a lot about those powerful and compelling elements of Jamaican society... This gives you some idea of the intermingling of cultural ideas going on, and we all benefited in our insights."

Punk was a common bond, he explained: "By this time, growing up as a black British youth, I was looking for something I could truly identify as my own, something which didn't act as some kind of mental or cultural straitjacket. I have to say, the young white kids, the punks, were very open to it too. We had our strong messages in the music... and the punks had their own strong message too, so there was a common ground in these respects. Listen to those early Pistols tunes. Both were interested in some kind of destruction and regeneration, a reinterpretation of the reality that had been presented to us."

Enter McLaren and Westwood and their Sex shop.

"Soon enough," Letts continues, "a lot of disenchanted, restless, guys were attracted to the shop, and these guys became a posse—a school of thought in their own way. John Lydon, Steve Jones, Joe Strummer, Paul Simonon—all of them would congregate there.

"So they were these upstarts, and we had some wild times. I would hold my corner, kicking out some heavy drum and bass dub tunes all day, burning spliffs. I was king of my space, and these white guys wanted to claim some space of their own, because of course, all the white guys were totally fed up with all those terrible rock bands that were around at the time, playing dreadful, arrogant, stadium rock. They wanted to deal a death blow to all those bands, and they went on to do that: for a while at least. They savaged those bands, totally deposed them. So for a lot of reasons, me and these upstarts, we all had a mutual respect for each other...

"Some of those guys were smarter than the others. John Lydon, for one. He just had a kind of vibe that attracted people to him, which I believe stemmed from the fact that he was aware of all he could be, not what he had been told he could be. Joe Strummer was smart too. These guys were the intelligentsia if you like, undoubtedly the brains behind what was emerging.

"Sid Vicious stood out too at that time... He wasn't the monster that the press made him out to be. In fact, I remember him as shy and quiet, gullible even. I remember time after time, he used to complain to us that he had been beaten up when he went out clubbing."

The next scene is another record signing—this time with A&M. A limo pulls up outside Buckingham Palace, spilling out the band and manager in front of a gaggle of invited press. Rotten emerges rubbing his jaw: as Temple recalled, the band had actually had a fight in the car as they arrived, with the singer taking the brunt of someone's ire, real or unintended. 'Bodies' plays in the background, and like a pack of scabrous dogs, the Pistols sign the deal, attended by numerous policemen. We know how it will all end, of course...

Lesson Six:

Become The World's Greatest Tourist Attraction

The most infamous episode in the Pistols' career—the Jubilee boat trip—is captured in riveting detail by Temple's camera. The standard studio video of 'God Save The Queen' is intercut with the necessarily rather shaky and wandering hand-held boat footage. As the director recalls, the Pistols hated being filmed and had perfected spitting into the camera lens from several feet away with pinpoint accuracy—but there's none of that here. The band are on a mission which precludes any larking about of this nature.

The boat departs and various onboard personnel are glimpsed, but after a couple of minutes the focus lands on the police who are waiting on the dock when it returns, having trailed it in their own boats beforehand. A scuffle of sorts ensues, with McLaren making the most vigorous protests: it takes two officers to drag him away. The other 10 arrests are either not shown or are only briefly glimpsed. A Top 10 radio countdown reveals the single's unjust fate: to remain at number two while deserving the top spot.

A brief animated section shows Lydon enduring the aftermath. His cartoon figure swaggers out of a pub and into a dark alleyway, where—in a touch of cinematic indulgence—he jumps in shock at a hidden noise before being set upon by three thugs. "God save the Queen, eh John?" mutters their neanderthal leader, before all three charge him with knives. Blood flows and the cartoon Rotten collapses to the ground. Temple had also suffered some public backlash on a personal level. He recalled later how once, while reading the *NME*, he was punched in the face, right through the paper.

Next we're taken to a video of 'Pretty Vacant,' which is interesting on several levels. It shows the Pistols as a more confident, and correspondingly insolent, act: Lydon doesn't feel the need to overplay the stylized aggression which he had made his on-stage trademark, and the air of restrained theatre behind the performance is gauged perfectly. But the real impact comes from Vicious, whose expertly communicated contempt is obvious. He is less camera-shy than in previous videos, and on this occasion his blank stare is both the essence of cool and a worrying look into the void.

In fact, Vicious emerges at this stage in the *Swindle* as an unexpectedly charismatic figure. This was perhaps by design (he was, after all, being groomed for stardom at this point, and Lydon's keen intelligence was hardly depicted in the movie) but also because he was a genuinely fascinating character. His biography has been told in great detail elsewhere (see *Further Reading*) but even those unfamiliar with his story will see the irony in the make-up of his character, just as his fellow Pistols did when they dubbed their mild-mannered friend Vicious. Yet the simple, placid fellow hidden behind the snarling exterior isn't the whole story: he had his dark edges too, exacerbated by the heroin that sank its teeth into him and refused to let go.

As he told Julien Temple, "The others just didn't understand you know. They thought, 'Oh, you can handle it!' But dope sickness isn't like that—it's not just something you can just blow away. Dope sickness is the worst sickness you can ever imagine: you can't get comfortable and you sweat. You're boiling hot and you pour with sweat. Then all of a sudden you get the colds and the sweat turns to fucking ice on you... You just can't win. You lie down, that's not comfortable. You sit up and that's not comfortable: it drives you insane... I don't want to be a junkie for the rest of my life. I don't want to be a junkie *at all*."

But a junkie was what Vicious had become by 1978, and there was, for him at least, no turning back. Temple added that in his view some people lacked a natural capacity to endure heroin. They could use it occasionally with few ill-effects, but Sid was not one of these.

Nonetheless, at this point in the movie he looks perfect: dark, angry and malevolent. As Lydon emphasizes the second syllable of 'vacant' with knowing obscenity, he looks like a prophet. In the background, Vicious resembles his subtler, more cautious nemesis...

Lesson Seven: Cultivate Hatred

... but not when it comes to his first solo spot, when he just looks like a yob.

Vicious's cover of Eddie Cochran's 'Something Else' is well sung and played, but the music isn't really the point. It's the accompanying visuals that grab the eye, and make the viewer realize just how much of a fully-fledged rock star he could have become.

Leaping off the bed in Boogie's London squat, Vicious is dressed only in a skimpy pair of Y-fronts, showing off his skinny buttocks. Acting the cartoon punk for all he's worth, he struts around the room, grabbing a beer from the fridge, gesticulating to Nancy—who sits on the bed, wearing the doe-eyed expression of the truly smacked-out—and then singing to himself in a full-length mirror. At one point he half-

The Sex Pistols: left to right, Sid Vicious, Steve Jones, Johnny Rotten, and Paul Cook.

John Lydon, aka Johnny Rotten, in 1978 around the time he left the Pistols on their 14-day American tour.

Johnny Rotten on stage during the US tour, which was a disaster from the start, ending in the group disbanding.

Sid Vicious on the US tour; when the band broke up, he stayed in New York until his death in early 1979.

Sid at the Winterland Ballroom, San Francisco 14 January 1978, Johnny Rotten's final gig with the band.

Drummer Paul Cook in 1978, sporting a promotional t-shirt for the Sex Pistols only album (apart from the Swindle soundtrack), Never Mind The Bollocks....

Steve Jones looking cool on stage during the American tour, shot by the prize-winning US photographer Lynn Goldsmith.

Malcom McLaren's
partner in the Sex
shop, designer
Vivienne Westwood,
here with Johnny
Rotten and celebrated
punk person Jordan

Edward Tudor-Pole
(who claimed to be
descended from Henry
VIII), who appeared in
the movie as Tadpole
the kiosk attendant.

The original Sex Pistols bass player, Glen Matlock, replaced by Sid Vicious in 1977.

Sid gives it the full-on angry teenager look in this still from The Great Rock'n'Roll Swindle.

The Pistols with McLaren (extreme right), signing their contract with A&M Records outside Buckingham Palace.

Malcom McLaren in a still from the movie, the making of which was his final association with the Sex Pistols.

Swindle *director Julien Temple in an 'Anarchy' shirt designed by* Vivienne Westwood *and Malcolm McLaren.*

Sid Vicious in a still from the movie, making his celebrated rendition of Frank Sinatra's 'My Way'.

Above: A scene from the film in which Sid Vicious mans a stall selling Sex Pistols 'God Save The Queen' ephemera.

Next page: The appropriately over-the-top poster for The Great Rock'n'Roll Swindle, *now a collector's item.*

STARRING

Sid Vicious

JOHNNY ROTTEN

Paul Cook

STEVE JONES

ence

BOYDS CO. & VIRGIN FILMS LIMITED

IN ASSOCIATION WITH MATRIXBEST LIMITED

PRESENT

THE GREAT ROCK 'N' ROLL SWINDLE

X

WITH MUSIC BY

SEX PISTOLS

WRITTEN & DIRECTED BY
JULIEN TEMPLE

EXECUTIVE PRODUCERS
JEREMY THOMAS & DON BOYD

WITH
Mary Millington

LIZ FRAZER

SPECIAL GUEST APPEARANCE

THE BLACK ARABS'

Irene Handl

RELEASED BY VIRGIN FILMS

McLaren

Helen of Troy

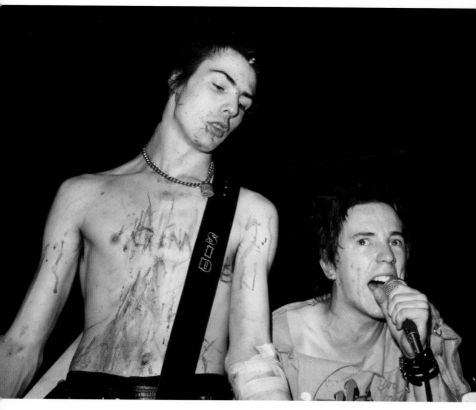

Vicious and Rotten in America, Sid's chest bleeding with self-inflicted razor-blade wounds reading 'Gimme a Fix'.

makes a self-cutting gesture with a broken beer bottle. His face is puffy, white and pocked with spots. His body is wasted and thin; his dancing is awkward. But he's an idol, all right.

All this overacting must have been pretty eye-opening stuff back in 1979, but after 26 years, *The Young Ones* and endless punk and post-punk posturing, the nihilism and catharsis that it represented back then seems diminished now. But if one thing is clear, it's that a solo career would have continued as it started—gloriously—although how long it could have continued is impossible to predict. Maybe Sid would have cleaned up and wised up, surviving alongside Iggy Pop to thrill us all with his post-narcotic tunes through the decades?

The action moves back to Steve Jones' rapidly tiring gumshoe, who now enters a brothel. As he walks towards its front door, a real-life tramp approaches him, obviously unaware that the scene is being filmed. It's a sign of the guitarist's confidence—or arrogance—as an actor that he dismisses the vagrant and continues the shot.

Once inside the brothel, Jones finds a prison cell—in complete darkness except for the cage in which the inmate sits and the prisoner himself, who is revealed as a record company executive seated at a desk. The actor playing him is Johnny Shannon, who had performed in the acclaimed Mick Jagger vehicle *Performance* and whom Temple wanted for a cameo role in *Swindle* in homage. Jones and Shannon's character spar verbally with each other, with the guitarist leaving in triumph as the latter breaks down in despair.

The *Performance* homage is apt, as the 1970 movie established a template for music film that stood the *Swindle* in good stead. In the Donald Cammell/Nic Roeg-directed film (in which a gangster played by James Fox seeks refuge in the guest house run by Jagger's faded rock star, Turner) we're shown a shadowy world where the underbelly of society is the point, not merely the milieu.

As punk icon Jayne County recalls: "In the traditional sense, *Performance* isn't a punk film. But in a wider definition, I suppose you could say it was punk. When it first came out, people saw it as a very decadent, perverted, almost scary sort of movie. It became a very cool and hip film to see. It separated the real freaks from the 'let's pretend we're freaks.' It got some very homophobic reactions as well. The hippies didn't get it, nor wanted to, but anyone who advocated revolution, upsetting society in general and tearing down the wall of repressed sexuality, loved the film. The 'bisexual' and 'androgynous' themes were a taste of what was just around the corner in pop culture—the glam movement."

Back in the *Swindle*, Jones is confronted with a series of doors, behind all of which some kind of sexual act—depraved, funny or otherwise—is going on. He half-heartedly slaps around a prostitute who can't or won't help him—the fisticuffs are comic rather than violent—and declaims: "I need to relax." Relaxation comes in the form of a tryst in one of the rooms, where a Japanese girl (Temple's girlfriend at the time) is lying invitingly on a bed surrounded by neon. Jones lies down next to her and they enact a comically fake sex scene.

Outside, Paul Cook—who has barely featured so far—pulls up in a car, looking for Jones. Simultaneously, a man with a snarling dog bursts into the room: surreally, the dog barks the instruction that McLaren has been seen heading towards Marylebone station. Jones leaps out of the window (the scene is becoming more like a *Carry On* movie by the second), joins Cook and the car takes off.

Now it's time for another solo effort from Vicious, and this time he offers a rendition of another Cochran classic, 'C'mon Everybody', while riding a motorbike, helmetless, down a series of country lanes. The song isn't particularly memorable, although it's interesting to see the bass player as happy as he seems to be here: there's no malevolence behind the performance. He's going, it emerges, to Paris...

We next cut to a platform at Marylebone, where McLaren is boarding a train. With a few words to Helen of Troy ("We were now a legend!") he departs. The train pulls into the distance as Jones and Cook run at full pelt after it—too late. He's gone.

Lesson Eight: Diversify Your Business

We're on the train. A rock star, styled as only a rock-star-hating punk band manager could style him, is sitting at ease. This is BJ, rather than MJ—the Mick Jagger on whom Temple had based him—as played by James Aubrey, an actor who had originally been signed up to work on the Meyer/Ebert version of the movie. Applying make-up and asking the guard that he be left in peace, BJ retires to a compartment.

His end is near. Sue 'Catwoman' Lucas, this time fully dressed, strangles him to death. The train has now pulled up at Northampton station and she leaps into a waiting car, making her escape accompanied by McLaren. The pair are just in time to avoid the boarding of the train by Steve Jones, who finds BJ's body with a rolling tape player jammed in his mouth. Removing the device, we hear McLaren's lectures coming from the speaker.

The death of the old, the arrival of the new? On a superficial level, of course. But there's more to this little scene than that. BJ's death at the hands of punk symbolizes the rise of the new guard and its simultaneous self-destruction: the punks committing sacrilege and in doing so leaving only their recorded legacy behind them. By this point in the filming process, the Pistols were long gone—and enough time would have passed for even those close to them to gain some perspective on their rapid-burning rise and fall. Bridges were burned by all the Pistols and their associates, and here's an apt metaphor for it.

Lesson Nine: Take Civilization To The Barbarians

The end is nigh. Temple's movie now takes us to America, where the Pistols are playing their doomed tour of conservative venues. Courtesy of footage shot on behalf of Warner Brothers, we immediately cut to Vicious on stage, standing resolute, bleeding, full of energy despite his addiction. He's staring down the crowd, blood dripping from his nose, onto his bare torso, onto his bass. It's car-crash filming. Local punks are interviewed, hilariously serious in their adulation—the exact adulation that McLaren and Temple wanted to wipe out. Meanwhile Steve Jones is aiming punches at the crowd, spitting at them and gesturing to them to come on stage and fight him.

It's down to Lydon to finish it off, and finish it he does, running out of energy and motivation during The Ramones' 'No Fun' and, psychotic stare well focused, delivers his 'Ever get the feeling you've been cheated?' kiss-off line. (His famous malevolent gaze was unintentional, as he told the author: "You must understand, I've always had bad eyesight. I have to stare to see what I'm looking at. It takes a long time for me to recognize what's going on. It's how I get detail. Sorry, there's no offence in it at all.")

The Pistols are dead. long live the Pistols! McLaren arrives at a run-down airfield to face the press, who have heard the news and, vulture-like, want to pick over the details. Holed up in a broken-down outbuilding near the apron are a small group of journalists, who are harangued by McLaren in the guise of answering their questions. "How much money has been made outta all of this?" demands an aggressive, bearded American. McLaren answers that the total so far is in the region of £695,000.

The day of the shoot was freezing, and McLaren shakes as he yells to make himself heard over the roar of a nearby taxiing airplane. "It's what I've dreamed of ever since I was 10 years old!" he screeches, before asking, "Who killed Bambi?"

Lesson Ten: Who Killed Bambi?
It's a rhetorical question, even if Temple muses "I think we all did." What can this question mean? Perhaps that we all share the guilt for everything that happens in this film, or to Sid and Nancy, or to punk, or to music, or to life in general. (A French film called *Who Killed Bambi?* [*Qui A Tué Bambi?*] was made in 2003, without any obvious reference to the Pistols.) But we're not told the answer, and we're not likely to be, either.

In the most grandiose, ambitious, section of Temple's slightly deranged movie, we are now taken to a softcore cinema in London's Piccadilly, where—we are informed via a series of lurid posters—a film called *The Great Rock 'n' Roll Swindle* is playing. Steve Jones is the main protagonist here, but Edward Tudor-Pole (who had made such a memorable entrance at the auditions for a new singer) puts in a show-stealing performance as an unhinged cinema usher. Singing the song 'Who Killed Bambi?' in a ridiculously exaggerated vaudeville sneer and handing out tickets to the cinema-goers, Tudor-Pole leaps from foot to foot, gurns ludicrously and is absolutely gripping.

McLaren had asked Tudor-Pole to write a song for the film. "He came round to my squat," he recalls, "and said, 'Ah right... yeah... hello. I want you to write a song called "Who Killed Bambi?"'" Then he said he would be back later: he was quite a funny bloke."

The co-writing credit with Vivienne Westwood came about because, Tudor-Pole says, "writing 'Who Killed Bambi?' was quite a long process. McLaren kept coming back and saying, 'I like that bit but I want that other bit better'... I wrote the lyrics but Vivienne improved upon some of the verse lyrics. Some of the lines in the verses are hers [but] I basically wrote it—in fact it's a rip-off of 'One Man Went To Mow,' isn't it?

"McLaren said they wanted to film me singing it, busking. So that's what I thought it was going to be—me and my guitar, singing this song we were trying to write. Then he changed his mind and said I should do it in the foyer as an usher, and we'll record it with a 45-piece orchestra!

"The next thing that happened, I'd written a version of the song, then McLaren came down with [Clash manager and long-time associate] Bernie Rhodes, who recorded it on his tape recorder, just me strumming in the basement of my squat. I don't know which version it was: it wasn't exactly the finished version. Then he said, 'I want you to meet the arranger, Andrew Pryce Jackman and he'll orchestrate it for the orchestra.' I met Andrew Pryce Jackman years later, he told me he never got paid!

"So I met the arranger and he said, 'You should definitely put an A in there,' I thought, 'Yeah, of course, thanks!' So he improved it another step. Then he did the orchestration for it, and the next thing was: 'Right, you're going to sing it next Wednesday—come down at six o'clock.. It was a big studio. Unfortunately, I didn't realise the orchestra were going to record it earlier, because I missed them. They'd had the 45-piece orchestra in and recorded it all. I turned up and they said, 'Listen to this!' I said, 'Right!' and started singing! Adrenaline, you know!"

The deranged vocals on the song weren't what Tudor-Pole had originally intended. It was McLaren who turned it into an exercise in extremity.

"I wanted to sing it quite well," he recalled, "[but] McLaren said, 'No, go more over the top.' He kept spurring me on: we did loads of takes. Take after take. 'More punk, more wild!' What happened was, he just saved all the most ridiculous bits from all the takes and put them all onto one track to make it sound as extreme as it could. Some bits make me really wince!"

As the song unfolds, Jones jumps the queue, grabs a ticket from the idiot usher and pushes past a row of seated film-watchers to find a seat, where he sits, stuffing himself with a box of chocolates. One of his neighbours is the singer Jess

Conrad and his girlfriend; another is Mary Millington. They watch as the on-screen action develops.

As a received-pronunciation newsreader (it's the voice of BBC legend John Snagge) is heard, we see the film within a film—the footage of Brazil that Temple shot in early 1978. Steve Jones (as himself) and Paul Cook visit the home of Train Robber Ronnie Biggs, an affable, tanned fellow in middle age who comes to his door with the query of "Have you bought an army with you?" He shakes hands with the two Pistols, who cheekily squeeze his flabby chest. We see the three head to the beach for a drink and some gratuitous shots of semi-naked Brazilian girls, plus a bevy of British tourists—"There were coachloads of tourists from Bolton," commented Temple dryly—and film of the Rio carnival.

The scenes with Biggs were controversial. To see one of the perpetrators of the Great Train Robbery at large and enjoying life must have raised the hackles of more than a few law-abiding citizens. Yet the three together seem rather tame. Ronnie asks Steve about the petty crime the guitarist had committed before joining the Pistols (the answer is stealing pens and pencils from Woolworth's) and admits he has squandered all the gains from the robbery 'down the boozer.'

Temple recalled of his time in Brazil that he was forced to stay much longer than originally planned, as some of the shooting required borrowed musical instruments that he had to return to their owners. He also had no money for weeks on end. McLaren endlessly promised to send it, but took a long time to do so. As a result Temple lived on fruit juice, eventually returning home in an incredibly healthy condition.

At this point the film slips into farce. Although the idea of filming Biggs is a masterstroke in terms of creating controversy, having him sing songs with the Pistols is a mistake. He does a remarkably good job of singing with them, but the movie's pace slows, the action is unfocused and the *Swindle's* previously acid-etched exposé of the Pistols myth descends into childish silliness. This is compounded by the appearance of Hitler's long-missing adjutant, Martin Bormann, played by an actor as a hint at the Nazi presence in South America in the 1970s. Temple also recalled that while they were in Brazil they would occasionally visit a lesbian strip club called Munich 21, which was attended by "all these ancient Nazis" with huge beer glasses.

We now cut back briefly to the cinema. Mary Millington, a slightly haggard-looking blonde, slips into the seat next to Steve and they begin a bout of kissing. Temple recalled her as a "sweet" person: she would commit suicide within months. Jess Conrad leaves in disgust, towing his girlfriend away and muttering the indistinct words "Come back Jess Conrad, all is forgiven."

On screen, Biggs is singing 'Belsen Was A Gas' with Jones and Cook. McLaren can be seen in the background, wearing sunglasses, a baseball cap and plasters on his face. The director later explained that the cuts had been caused by a car crash immediately after arriving in Brazil: the team had hired a Volkswagen Beetle which Steve promptly crashed, sending Malcolm through the windscreen. As he recovered beneath his cap and bandages, many Brazilians thought he was Niki Lauda, the racing driver who had been burned badly on the face and scalp in an accident just 18 months before, and called him 'Niki.' Surreal? The truth as much as the film, apparently.

The *Swindle* reaches its nadir with the scene of Cook, Jones, Biggs and 'Bormann' perched precariously on a boat on the Amazon. All four perform, while the boat rocks but the scene isn't controversial (the idea of Biggs and Nazis on the run in Brazil is established by now), musical, or in any way necessary. Temple himself admitted that he lost focus with these scenes.

Back in the cinema, Jones and Millington are grappling with each other in earnest. Usherette Irene Handl is disapproving, entering the foyer to inform Tudor-Pole of the goings-on. By now there is an on-screen intermission. Adverts for Rotten chocolate bars, a soft drink called Anarkee-Ora and the Vicious Burger accompany the off-screen activity, which now consists of Millington fellating Jones.

But the climactic scene (no pun intended) has arrived. With utter insolence, Sid Vicious is seen swaggering his way down a Paris street and into a series of scrapes. He leers into the window of a restaurant, shocking two elderly ladies with his appearance—the spiked black hair, the boots, the swastika: they're all in place. He enters a patisserie and buys a large strawberry and cream gateau: an assistant runs after him and he writes his autograph on the front of her white work coat. Most shockingly, a friendly woman—prostitute or otherwise, we do not learn—beckons him over to a street corner: he goes to talk to her and then slams the entire cake in her face with sobering violence. Watch the scene again: it doesn't look as if the actress playing the part was expecting to be hit as hard as that.

After buying a gun from a suitably dodgy dealer, Vicious stumbles off. There's a short break back in the cinema as

Tudor-Pole and Handl exchange dialogue in the cinema foyer. And then it comes, the magnificent, apocalyptic, scene in which Vicious—dressed in white dress jacket—performs a version of Frank Sinatra's 'My Way.'

The song—which he delivers with an initial overblown, piss-taking impression of Frank's showbiz croon, before adopting a Rotten-style punk snarl—is to this day the recording for which Vicious is most remembered. The image of Vicious snarling into the microphone, dress jacket flapping, is also iconic. The scene was indeed set for his solo career, although—as Temple recalled—by this stage he too had fallen out with McLaren, demanding that the manager release him from his contract.

Filmed in an empty cinema—apart from the film crew and, bizarrely, the singer Serge Gainsbourg (who had just filmed there himself; he is said to have loved Sid's song), 'My Way' is interspersed with shots of an audience, most of whom applaud his song with delight. In the front row sits Sid's mother Ann Beverly.

It's an inspired performance. Partially rewritten with Sid's own lyrics (he addresses a childhood guilt with the line "I killed a cat"), 'My Way' takes on a new meaning, one which cultural analysts have decided ever since is nothing less than a malevolent celebration of the triumph of punk over its obsolete predecessors. Well, maybe they're right. But it's also a fine piece of music-making in its own right, with the backing—Cook and Jones—and the arrangement of strings plus punk guitar a thing of beauty.

As the song spirals to a close with ascending orchestral flourishes and Sid's triumphant snarls, he draws his gun and shoots people in the audience. The crowd scream and panic; he turns and lopes away up the stairs at the back of the stage—not to be seen again on screen, and without much of a future off it either. Perhaps the stairs, upwards into the light, is a metaphor... or perhaps that's going too far. Either way, the theme of shooting the audience ties in perfectly with the motive behind the *Swindle*: to annoy, disillusion and ultimately remove the fans and their misplaced worship of the Pistols, who—by the time the film was seen—had long since removed themselves anyway.

Steve Jones is now seen holding up two cardboard tablets, on which are etched the 10 lessons above. Laughter breaks out as the camera pulls back: he throws them on the floor and we see that he is half naked, with his genitals exposed. It's a suitably meaningless, negative, image to end on.

Or almost end on. There's a couple of minutes of comedy animation to endure—this time of the Pistols' obscene take on the traditional 'Friggin' In The Riggin'.' A pirate ship bobs on the waves: the captain, Malcolm McLaren, pushes John Lydon off a plank at the point of a sword. Lydon, no doubt unfairly, is seen gasping in terror— and is consumed by a ravenous shark with 'Virgin' written on its side. The ship begins to sink. Vicious leaps from the side, knife in hand. As the whole, sorry, vessel slips beneath the waves, we're left with McLaren, who salutes before he too is drawn under.

The very last images—a montage of newspaper cuttings displaying headlines about Vicious' death—sits motionless on screen for several seconds. There were added at the 'request,' said Temple, of the industry censors, the British Board of Film

Classification. "They wanted the Victorian morality ending," sighs the director.

And so the *Swindle* swindles itself to a close.

Now we know what's in the film, what isn't in it? After all, the movie was driven—at least until McLaren's withdrawal, a long way down the line in the editing process—by a man with an agenda. This agenda focused on the promotion of Sid Vicious as a solo star, and it also took great care to fire some slightly nasty shots towards John Lydon, who had turned up his nose at it, and by implication at the Pistols.

The first big gap is a Glen Matlock-shaped one. The writer of most of the Pistols' biggest and most lucrative hits, the original bassist left the band to be replaced by the more photogenic Sid, although he did subsequently play on the *Never Mind The Bollocks...* album. He's seen in the warehouse party footage from 1975, but otherwise he's a spectral presence despite his bass playing all over the songs.

"We decided that everything would be a four-way split, which maybe wasn't a good business move in the long run, but there you go," he recently told one interviewer, being pragmatic about the enormous loss of earnings this represented to him, especially on songs such as 'Pretty Vacant' which he wrote single-handedly. But his conformity to the standard, non-subversive rock 'n' roll way didn't fit in with McLaren's 1978-79 vision of the Sex Pistols, so he wasn't included as a result.

The second major omission is *Never Mind The Bollocks... Here's The Sex Pistols*, the band's only real album and an essential recording of its day. Although most of the songs it contained are played at some point in the movie—some in several versions, such as the French street musicians' version of 'Anarchy' for violin and accordion—and the cover is briefly shown being burned on McLaren's fire, there's little serious analysis of what the record meant, why its title was so controversial and how it was produced.

Yet there could have been so much in the film about the LP, beginning with that title. Needless to say, on the album's release the use of the word 'bollocks' caused endless upset, despite the fact that the Pistols could have been much more profane if they'd chosen to be. As Lydon said, "In the early Pistols days, I was openly debated in parliament under the Traitors Act. I had to fight legal battles over the word 'bollocks' and the right to use it, while I was facing a jail sentence for blasphemy. I was the one who wrote it, so I faced it personally."

Artist Jamie Reid explained the underlying reason for the problem: "The vagrancy and obscenity laws in Britain [are] left over from the Napoleonic wars, when all the soldiers came back to Britain. No jobs, nowhere to live, so people were on the streets, and they brought in those laws about palm-reading, astrology, vagrancy, obscenity, prostitution. Those laws still exist and they relate back to those times. But I mean, the Pistols... [the obscenity was] far less significant actually than the look, the fashion, the sleeves, the music, and the attitude—which was like, 90 percent of it—which went off in all sorts of directions and changed culture quite fundamentally."

Of the famous magenta and yellow design for the *Never Mind The Bollocks* sleeve—perhaps the single most iconic punk image—Reid recalled: "A bit of a nightmare with printers on this one. The yellow in particular is extremely difficult to print, as any impurities are actually emphasized in the process. As for the color scheme, there weren't any hidden meanings or symbolism in the colours used; they just 'worked' together as a design, eventually. On release, the cover was criticized for being both 'shoddy', plus there was no band picture anywhere within the design. Despite this, *Rolling Stone* voted it number two best LP cover—*Sgt. Pepper* took the number one slot.

"As for today, there are still echoes of the 'style' to be seen everywhere, from high-street banks to [TV show] *Never Mind The Buzzcocks*. I have always been happy to see these graphics imitated, though obviously there are good and bad imitations."

There's also a large gap in the form of Vivienne Westwood—especially given her close relationship with McLaren, and her involvement in the look of the Pistols and their coterie. Nowadays Westwood is an international fashion brand in perfume as well as clothing, and retains much punk kudos despite her slightly startling resemblance to Margaret Thatcher. Much respect is due to her. As she once recalled, "Malcolm and I created punk rock fashion, which we sold in our shop and which was promoted through the Sex Pistols. Who knows what would have happened without this combination of events?"

Of the introduction of the swastika into the Pistols' clothing—a move that was even more shocking then that it is now—she reasoned: "Nazism is politically embedded in our history and it is still there, spreading like an oil stain in a society that worships business. The Sex Pistols gained notoriety by shocking, and it was Malcolm McLaren—who is Jewish on his mother's side—who introduced the swastika into the iconography of the group. The statement was: if your civilization produces Nazis then that civilization is rubbish."

Westood's story is one that really should have been told in the movie. As she explained, she and McLaren had "wanted to make a stand against the American involvement in the Vietnam War and in the process be part of the youth rebellion... What changed our lives forever was when Malcolm had the idea to sell rock 'n' roll records to trendy customers. No one ever heard rock 'n' roll on the radio at the time. We not only discovered the appeal of the records, but the second wave of teddy boys who were creating their own excitement in the East End.

"We were looking for a market stall to sell these records, but couldn't find one. There was a little shop, however, on King's Road that was going bust. It was the first shop that sold used denim, but nobody was into it. The owners invited us to have a bit of their shop. We moved into the back, made it into a little 1950s sitting room and started to sell the records. We had an immediate success. For one thing, these teddy boys were thrilled to buy the records."

Of the shop at 430 King's Road—which she took over and renamed World's End—Westwood said: "What it meant for me was that I always had direct access to the public, right from the beginning of designing clothes. I was always able to test my ideas by selling them direct. My company has the same identity today. I've never had businessmen telling me what to do.

"Having that outlet, my shop, was very important to me. For example, I never had a sale in that shop. The ideas were strong, but there weren't so many of them. For example, if

I had one or two great pairs of trousers, I didn't need ten in those days. We did start by making a lot of money. But this didn't continue, because soon after I had a manager who stole for many, many years. After I discovered it, my business started to grow. So, it was a good idea having a shop for me. It gave me a way to work where I wasn't under pressure, where I could develop my ideas and technique."

If it seems shallow that clothes bore so much of the message of punk, consider the following statement by sometime Ants member Marco Pirroni: "It was individuals—individuals who didn't fit and didn't wanna fit. We're the one per cent who don't fit, don't care. Then you go to the shop and you meet these funny people who encourage you... That's what I thought the clothes were all about—attack! It was like 'I live in this world which I fucking hate. Every day I'm bombarded by visual images I can't stand, by television I can't stand, by music I can't stand, by trousers I can't stand, by hair I can't stand. So I'm going to wear this T-shirt, I'm going to wear these clothes, I'm going to wear these fucking pointed shoes, and this is my attack, my revenge."

Bromley Contingent regular Siouxsie Sioux once explained: "Before we were on the Bill Grundy show with the Pistols and before punk had been seized on by the tabloids, there was a healthy fear of our [punks'] appearance. And it's funny how that fear turned to hatred once the phenomenon had been identified—or was considered to have been identified—and contained. When I hired a costume from Berman's & Nathan's to go and see Roxy Music at Wembley Arena in 1975 (it was a cross between a mermaid and a chorus girl—purple sequins with a fish-tail train), I didn't get changed in the toilets at Charing Cross station. I travelled up to town in that outfit. I got odd looks, but if they saw you looking they'd turn away. I think that people sense that kind of single-mindedness and don't dare approach you. But all that really did change once punk was picked up on in the media. Then the public reaction was abusive.

"Looking back on those days, nothing can really capture quite how out on a limb the primary people were," she added. "How brave it was, I suppose—without it really seeming brave at the time; more a kind of recklessness. But the term 'punk' was so lazy and easy and inaccurate. The Pistols were different because they had Rotten—without him, who knows? And The Clash went at it in a way that was far more traditional—a kind of Keith Richards thing. I wasn't trying to be masculine and getting down with the boys, so the main difference between us and the rest was that it wasn't a solely male perspective. I think a certain amount of anger has been a fuel of mine, if you want—but also some sort of sadness, and plain mischief, of course."

The violence that the punk scene attracted in what NME dubbed 'The Summer of Hate' is also not really addressed. Although Lydon is slashed with a knife in cartoon form and McLaren is dragged away by police officers with a rather unusual degree of force, the malevolent brutality that characterised some of the gigs and events is skirted around.

As Slits bassist Tessa Pollitt once reported to 3AM magazine, "Sometimes things got really intense. People ask if we were ever subjected to violence. Let me tell you, please document how many times we were harassed by people. It's hard to count how many times. I remember one time, the

Pistols were playing at The Screen On The Green, Islington. In the foyer, this guy came up to us, came up behind [Slits singer] Ari Up and said, 'So you're The Slits? Well, here's a slit for you' and he just shoved a knife into her backside. Sliced her butt, quite literally, right there. Luckily for Ari, she was wearing so many layers of clothes, the damage was limited. It just seemed to others that we were asking for it. The vibe towards us was, 'Know your place, woman'! It seemed that we couldn't go anywhere without getting a reaction from people. The attitude was that we were asking for it, but we certainly weren't asking anyone to come up behind us with a knife.

"Another time we went to a sound system blues dance, as we did so often at that time, but on this one particular occasion I remember, someone took offence at what we were, how we looked, and chose to push a huge bass speaker stack right onto us. We just got out of the way in time. Women looking like we did, walking in with the rebel dread Don Letts, sometimes people just couldn't accept it. You see, one thing I'd like to stress is, The Slits always had a sense of humor, a sense of the ridiculous, and some people just did not get it. They took it so seriously, and we got it in the neck."

The movie also chooses not to tackle the drug that was responsible for so much damage, on the punk scene and elsewhere—heroin. Much could have been said on the subject, as Tessa Pollitt said: "It seems to me that London was flooded with heroin around the time punk was losing direction, and it seems to me to be too much of a coincidence. It almost felt to me as if there was a conspiracy to sedate people. London was just flooded with it, and a lot of us were affected by it. I've said this before, and I'll say it again. It's just something that I feel. The tail-end of punk saw the market swamped. Governments have done it in the past to quiet things down. Shove a load of drugs in, shut people up. I noticed so many people affected by it. Sid Vicious was affected by it—he died because of it.

"You have to be careful talking about heroin and the punk era," she added. "People romanticize it. There is nothing whatsoever that is romantic about heroin: it is medicine for those suffering a painful death. It has a history of sedative control in warfare too. A later manifestation of that government control would be the acid and ecstasy scene in the 1980s which left me cold, spooked me out, gave me a chill, and it was around that time that I lost interest in what was going on in London musically."

And finally, John Lydon is only present on previously recorded footage and in animated form. The movie lacked its most important proponent, therefore, and suffers as a result. As Temple later told *Record Collector*, "The film's big flaw is that John Lydon didn't get involved, due to the breakdown of relations with Malcolm."

Lydon himself explained in an interview with the author in the same magazine that his relationship with McLaren was beyond negative—it was practically poisonous. "He's a silly man: he started to believe his own Svengali nonsense. It was a good mind game, and we used to get on all right with each other until he started to believe all that as a genuine form of existence—and it isn't. He always tends to copy someone: he did it with Andy Warhol, 'I'm a living monument'... all preposterous, and it's been done better. That's where he goes wrong."

The manager, alleged Lydon, had also neglected to help his band out of a sticky situation. "Malcolm would never, ever, *ever* be around when there was a problem. Not never, ever. But he was there to collect the awards! He was always very jealous of me, and I think he always will be... Because he wanted the credit. But he doesn't have the talent or the brains to create these things. Not that I care, but it is fact and I'd be a fool to deny it. And knowing it hurts him like hell is all the more enjoyable!"

As Temple put it: "The idea that the band couldn't play—which was nonsense—was obviously the product of his myth-making mischief. Malcolm was saying that he was the puppetmaster who modelled these clay figures into animate beings, pulling the strings on everything they did. And completely diminishing the roles of people like John and Steve, which was absurd when you consider their experience and background, and where they came from and how they'd fought to be who they were."

After this many years, we can see McLaren's intentions behind *The Great Rock 'n' Roll Swindle* for what they are—basically a celebration of himself and those he favored, as well as an exercise in iconoclasm—and react in the way that people have always reacted to him. That is, with a mixture of distrust (he is a manipulator extraordinaire, according to those who have been close to him) and reluctant admiration (he was, after all, a significant cultural catalyst with some original ideas). But would audiences in 1980, when it was still all so fresh and shocking, see the wood for the trees?

the movie that would not die

"The punters bought it—hook, line, and sinker"

Steve Jones

Steve Jones was once asked if the enormous public antipathy towards the Pistols—embodied by the stuffed-shirt presenter in the *Swindle* who announces that "the Sex Pistols would be vastly improved by sudden death"—ever worried him. His reply was both perspicacious and sanguine: "At the time, it was genius, just because you couldn't buy publicity like that. Even though we didn't deliberately go on to shock anyone, the mainstream bullshit papers latched on to it." It was, as he added, an entirely new way of approaching the public: "Back then it was a big deal. No one had ever really tapped into that. It hadn't been done before. Everyone was wearing flares and clogs!"

He was right. No one had been in the position of a film audience being mocked by the actual film they were watching. The filmed auditioning singers, the lessons so callously dealt out by McLaren, the objectification of the Bromley Contingent (Sue 'Catwoman' Lucas, a pubescent teenager, being scrawled on; Jordan being stripped on stage by Lydon) and the self-elevation of McLaren ('Bring civilization to the barbarians')—all spoke of a dislike of, even a disdain for, the fans who had made the Pistols a phenomenon.

Such bridge-burning was unknown in the movie or musical world in 1980. Julien Temple: *"The Great Rock 'n' Roll Swindle* was obviously doing something that no other pop film had done by then, which was not to worship or make a hagiography out of the band. It was more complex than that. I wanted to undercut the sense of worship that had grown up around the Pistols, which in the beginning they'd set out to destroy. We were inspired by Orson Welles' *F For Fake* when we were writing it, which deliberately falsified things, turned things on their head and forced you to believe all kinds of stuff."* (Temple is referring to Welles' *Vérités Et Mensonges*, a 1974 documentary in which the celebrated actor-director addressed the subject of fakery and played games with the audience at the same time.)

Consider the movies that were released at about the same time as the *Swindle*. Big-grossing films of 1979 included feelgood weepies (*Kramer Vs. Kramer, The Black Stallion*) and sub-*Star Wars* sci-fi fare such as *Star Trek: The Motion Picture* and *The Black Hole*. Intellectual comedies such as *Manhattan* were the talk of the film literati. In 1980, audience-pleasing escapism such as *Any Which Way You Can, Popeye* and *Nine To Five* was the order of the day, while behemoths such as *The Empire Strikes Back* and *Superman II* made this little punk film—produced for a now-microscopic £250,000—a tiny minnow in a huge lake.

Temple looked back on the *Swindle* with affection. Although it was hardly the toast of the critics then or since ("We had a mixed reaction," he offered diplomatically), he felt quite rightly that its audience were left alienated by it, achieving its intended aim. "They loved it and hated it at the same time. But by that time the Sex Pistols had ended and there was blood all over the walls. No one was really talking and certainly John and Malcolm weren't."

"We certainly incited fans to strange acts in the cinema," he told *Record Collector*. "In Paris, we had the premiere at some huge old art deco theatre and they got into the projection booth and ripped the projector bolts out, so that the film was flying all over the ceiling. In Hamburg, during Sid's 'My Way' sequence, they sprayed lighter fuel all over the screen and set fire to it. In London, a kid who was the spitting image of Sid—white dinner jacket, motorbike boots and talcum powder—jumped out with a gun underneath the screen and started firing blanks at the audience."

Temple also recalled that his hero, the French director Jean-Luc Godard, had enjoyed the *Swindle*. "He told me he loved it. He called the way it was edited 'the future of film,' That was amazing. Soon after he said that, we were both attending a film festival and I saw him sitting at a café by himself. I walked up to him and said: 'Mr. Godard?' and he said: 'Fuck off.' That was all he said. That's the way heroes behave!"

Many of the Pistols' contemporaries liked the film, or at least began to like it after a few years had passed and its malevolent heart was tempered a little by nostalgia and by the public's growing sophistication. Adverts singer TV Smith recalls: "It was an enjoyable piece of candy floss, but left the impression with a lot of people that 'this was how it happened.' It wasn't, and left a bit of a sour taste in the mouth the way Malcolm re-invented the Pistols story with himself as the sole star. I was a lot happier about the whole thing after Julien Temple made *The Filth And The Fury*, which was a much more informed look at the whole period."

Jake Burns of Stiff Little Fingers explains: "With the *Swindle*, Malcolm McLaren did what he set out to do, which was to shock, shake up and exploit a moribund music industry that had lost sight of its core audience—young rebellious folks!

"I think the Pistols were important in so much as they were the spearhead of a hugely influential youth movement—one that reverberates right up to the present day. While they may not have been the first punk band— there was The Ramones, and so on—they were the guys who brought the whole thing to nationwide attention. The Pistols broke down the walls for just about every worthwhile rock band that followed. Had it not been for them—and all the prejudice they worked through—we would have been condemned to years of nothing but 'Yes, it's a Genesis-speedwagon-styx-collins band.' You have to be grateful for that. I don't think any new punk band has recorded anything as acerbic or threatening as 'God Save The Queen.' Rock 'n' roll is supposed to be loud, uncouth and raucous. I'm glad he wasn't our manager, though..."

Jayne County holds a different opinion. "I think Malcolm did a brilliant job on the Pistols. I would give anything for him to manage me. He was relentless! He got them to write some great songs, and got them rocking. Even if the sound was a reworking of Johnny Thunders and the New York Dolls, the themes were different and they were more snotty and snarling. It worked even if Malcolm did basically manufacture them. He was of the 'all PR is good' school— and in this case Malcolm took the 'bad' and made it work like nobody else ever had. The worse the PR the better it was. Shock and outrage gets attention—I should know!"

Dave Parsons of Sham 69 muses: "What I found interesting was how offended everyone got. I think the whole point was that if you were offended you were missing the point—or playing into the hands of The Embezzler. When you do Tai Chi as a martial art you use the aggressor's anger and power against themselves—and in a way that's what McLaren was doing with the *Swindle*. I don't know if on the one hand it's a particularly good film, but on the other it's a work of art, even taking into account the fact that most of the scenes are re-enactments of other films."

As for McLaren, Parsons adds: "I admired McLaren's vision and audacity, from the New York Dolls to the completion of the film. Let's face it, without him punk might not have happened, even if his view of punk wasn't the same as ours. He did a good job of looking after himself and successfully taking his project to fruition, although a good manager should have the interests and care of the band members as a priority, which McLaren obviously didn't."

Jayne County again: "I found it to be a very entertaining film, certainly more entertaining than, say, Derek Jarman's *Jubilee*. It didn't try to be a work of art—it was childish and irreverent at the same time. I think the film let you know that it was all basically a farce. They were taking the piss out of everyone, especially the recording industry—which was a joke by then anyway. The film was the ultimate rock 'n' roll parody. And the idiots who say punk wasn't rock 'n' roll don't know their asses from their anal canals—it was rock 'n' roll, not unlike the Dolls, Chuck Berry or The Rolling Stones for that matter—just played with a super-snotty attitude and with a special 'Fuck you!' for everyone! It made it all seem new, but anyone who knows rock 'n' roll history knows that real rock 'n' roll was like that anyway—rebellious, snotty and threatening! I think the film made that point well.

"And the thing I liked best about it was that it sent itself up—Malcolm was saying: OK, The Who sang 'Won't Get Fooled Again'—but ha ha, they did! The Pistols, as good a band as they were, were the brainchild of Malcolm—they were not a band who'd been playing around forever and then all of a sudden Malcolm found them and all that. He actually put them together. It was totally calculated!"

I put this theory to Lydon in 2005. "Really?" he snarled. "Like he invented me? When he walked into me, he didn't know what he was taking on. I think the same thing about Steve and Paul and Glen and Sid. He didn't know what he was getting into... I see Malcolm occasionally. I feel sorry for him now, he's like a sad old lady. He's allowed himself to get bitter and twisted with life, and you shouldn't do that. Heaven is on this earth: this is all we know. Not that dream vision stuff after death: I'm not sure that any of that exists. You better enjoy what you have here, so if you put yourself in your own prison mentality, there's not much left for you."

Back to Jayne County. Does she think the film achieved its aims? "I think it comes pretty close," she agrees. "There are moments when it seems they are just acting out what people expect of them—going through the motions of 'bad behavior' just to create and keep the myth of the Pistols going. But then again, a lot of the myth-making was based on reality. Alcohol had a lot to do with it as well. And poor Sid of course felt pressured to act like a retarded maniac, when actually in real life he was a pussycat—a real sweetie!

"The film reminded me of some of Andy Warhol's films, where it got kind of difficult to really tell if they were being serious or not. It was like, 'Let's see how far we can push this, before people catch on!' It's fun sending up the establishment while at the same time making money doing it, and pulling the wool over everyone's eyes, while at the same time making what you are doing hip. That is what real pop art is. And what we can get away with if you can convince people that what you are doing is art! Make 'normal' people feel cool, and they will give you money and everyone is happy."

McLaren and Temple pushed their concept almost as far as it would go, accompanying their semi-spoof film with a semi-spoof soundtrack album. *The Great Rock 'n' Roll Swindle* album was the Pistols' second LP in name, although it doesn't really qualify as such due to its cobbled-together nature. There are alternate versions of established Pistols songs, songs that had already appeared on *Never Mind The Bollocks... Here's The Sex Pistols*, unimpressive covers, songs by other artists such as The Black Arabs and even some extra songs— 'Here We Go Again' and 'Black Leather'—that hadn't made it into the movie. Nonetheless, it has its high points—Sid Vicious' still-excellent version of 'My Way', the Tudor-Pole/ Westwood orchestral lunacy of 'Who Killed Bambi?' and the strings version of 'EMI,' although all Pistols fans will have their own preferences. Few listeners, however, will spare much time on the Ronnie Biggs/Martin Bormann tracks or Vicious' generic Eddie Cochran covers.

And so the *Swindle* landed in the public's laps, in visual and audio form. Critics were largely unmoved or indifferent, but in this case—almost uniquely—it was the public's reaction that counted, as the movie was made for them and them alone. As the fans gradually woke up to the fact that their idols were being methodically desecrated on the screen in front of them, some dismissed it, others felt betrayed and a significant number loved it. To this day the reactions are mixed. Lydon would have been pleased, ironically: *The Great Rock 'n' Roll Swindle* is a film that requires the watcher to make an independent decision.

Of course, the *Swindle* wasn't the first film to have caused extreme reactions among its audience, but it was the first to have taunted them so mercilessly. By the 1980s most people were open to the idea of cinema as instigator of cultural change. After all, the *Swindle* was merely the latest in a line of 'rock films' that presented a more or less establishment-scaring view. From the harmless but cleverer-than-people-thought wordplay of *A Hard Day's Night* via The Monkees' *Head* and *Slade In Flame*, there had been a tradition of mockery and vaudeville when music met celluloid. *The Great Rock 'n' Roll Swindle* was, we now know, the latest and most calculating of the bunch—and has not been superceded in intelligence or the accuracy of its targeting to this day, despite worthy cinematic efforts in modern times by Metallica, Portishead and The Rolling Stones.

Let us not forget the importance of the *Swindle* in the environment of its day. Two years earlier or two years later, it might not have tapped into the nation's consciousness quite as deeply as it did. As Jamie Reid told *Skrufff*: "It was perfect timing, with that first generation of kids coming out of school, particularly working-class kids, who'd been given loads of promises but had nothing to do, whether jobs or opportunities. It was all about that do-it-yourself, fuck-all-that-fucking-corporate-glam-rock-shit that was going on in the music business. We did our own artwork, produced our own music and the whole thing was inspirational. Punk was also very tribal, which was interesting and in its own way, quite pacifist. It wasn't about the icons such as the Pistols or The Clash, or whoever. I know from being a visual artist involved in campaigns such as the Criminal Justice Bill and the Poll Tax that it's about a continuous story of protest."

In fact, the *Swindle's* only real rival in the punk movement—although the movies have differing agendas—is *Jubilee*, Derek Jarman's 1977 exercise in social commentary through surrealism. In the film—set initially in the year 1578, 400 years before the then-present day—Queen Elizabeth I asks her court magician, Dr. John Dee, to give her a vision of events yet to come. The angel Ariel appears and takes her to the England of the far future.

It's a hideous place: a wasteland where civilization has stagnated. Gangs of punks roam the streets, battling the fascist police state. Buckingham Palace is a recording studio, the hub of an entertainment empire owned by media tyrant Borgia Ginz. Characters fighting his forces include the historian Amyl Nitrite (played by Pamela 'Jordan' Rooke), the firestarter Mad (Toyah Willcox), the actress Crabs (Little Nell of *Rocky Horror* fame), brothers Sphinx and Angel, the artist Viv and a nanny called Chaos. Music comes from a suitably punkish cast including Siouxsie & The Banshees, Chelsea, Wayne (not yet Jayne) County & The Electric Chairs and a pseudonymous Adam & The Ants.

Jubilee is a well-realised if slightly self-indulgent flight of fancy and homage to punk by Jarman. It appeals to aesthetes rather than actual punk fans—but it's the only piece of art that comes near to *The Great Rock 'n' Roll Swindle* in shape or content. As years passed and the 'punk era'—with its first wave falling approximately into 1976-81—became more distant, the two films merged in some observers' awareness as 'the punk film scene' despite their vast differences. How time heals all...

Was the *Swindle* itself an influence on future music—the next incarnation of punk? Jayne County thinks so. "Just as *Performance* influenced a lot of people including me and the New York Dolls and so on, the Pistols' film influenced all the future Green Days. Kids who missed punk the first time around could now take part in a movement that, in actuality, was already gone.

"We had New Wave forced on us by the established recording industry because real punk was too scary and threatening. Just as the recording industry of the 1950s destroyed real rock 'n' roll by watering down black music and having squeaky-clean white kids singing the cleaned-up, less threatening versions—rough and raw became smooth and overcooked!—rock 'n' roll was swept under the rug like dirt and replaced by tailor-made recording industry puppets. The Pistols' film will always be a testimony of what real rock 'n' roll can and should be."

She adds: "This film was the ultimate put-down of all the bullshit that the recording industry always puts rock 'n' roll music through in order to water it down and make more money for themselves. Punk, which was a made-up word for the music anyway—a word that was used in prison for the boy who gets fucked up the ass—was *real* rock 'n' roll. Punk was the new, realer, version of rock 'n' roll!"

The label 'punk' is often thought, as County affirms, to be an import of dubious origin, but many disagree. As Tessa Pollitt of The Slits said, "Punk to me wasn't an American thing at all, it was a very British thing. According to so many people, it all started off when Malcolm McLaren went over to America and linked up with the New York Dolls, but punk is just a word. Punk would've happened anyway: whatever else it would have been called, it was inevitable. Malcolm McLaren has taken far too much credit for it. There was a whole undercurrent going on, and something was about to explode back in 1976. Something just *had* to explode..."

What did the Pistols actually signify, when all was said and done?

Jayne County: "The Pistols signalled a change of the guard. It meant redefining rock in general and respecting rock 'n' roll's roots. Simple chords, a good beat and I give it a 99! They and the whole punk scene let the kids know that anyone can be in a band. You gotta have the guts and the nerve to stand up to the established norm, and say 'Enough shit!' Real rock 'n' roll has always had to fight to stay alive, because so many assholes out there would love to see it just fade away but it won't!

"The Pistols were a major battle, but unfortunately they didn't win the war. We are still having to fight to keep real rock 'n' roll alive. The war will go on forever, although every once in a while we have a rock 'n' roll resurrection. The punk movement was one, the glam, the hippy, the rockabilly, the alternative scene and so on—the bones just keep right on a-rising!"

And of course, there's still the Pistols' shocking, always relevant music to enjoy. As County enthuses, "The music stands up like a stick in a can of dried paint! Like Dusty Springfield's hair in a hurricane... It is there and it cannot be knocked down. It sounds better today that it did years ago, because the music scene today is totally controlled by the record companies. Everything is watered down for mass consumption. Totally overproduced and machine washed. Just about all old rock 'n' roll and punk sounds great today. Better than ever. That's why so many people including kids are turning back the clock to when music was real, threatening and fun!"

So who won the War Of The Swindle? Was it the musicians, the fans, the industry or the general public?

Sid Vicious died more than a year before the movie even appeared, one of the first of an ever-growing pantheon of punk dead alongside his beloved Nancy. The industry didn't finish him off—he managed that all by himself. In due course Spungen's mother Deborah wrote a book about the trials she had endured, in which she stated that her daughter had suffered from paranoid schizophrenia. The sad story of Vicious and Spungen was eventually turned into an off-Broadway play and a well-received movie, simply titled *Sid And Nancy*, starring Gary Oldman and directed by Alex Cox.

Despite his image as a drug-addict and knife-wielder, Sid Vicious inspired a great deal of affection. As Tessa Pollitt of The Slits said: "I feel upset when I read all the nonsense people write about Sid now. Sid was always one of my favorite people, and he was a gentle soul. Him and John just really complemented each other. I think of Sid as very gentle, and now I see he was a victim, a victim of Malcolm McLaren, a victim of Nancy Spungen too. Nancy travelled around with us on one of our tours. I just can't put into words what I think about Nancy!

"Sid was gentle, you know, and he was just used up in the end. To me he epitomized the spirit of what punk was, and he had a lot of humor! I'm always looking for humor in people, and looking into their intention. He was hilarious, like a kid, like a cartoon figure. He also had a vulnerability and naivety that I look for in people, something pure. He had that purity. Definitely. I think it deeply affected John to lose Sid as a friend. I'm sure of it."

She wasn't wrong. At one point in Julien Temple's 2000 revisitation of the Pistols story, *The Filth And The Fury*, Lydon reveals with jaw-dropping sincerity the depth of his hurt at Vicious' death. "I feel guilty about Sid: I wish I could have told him more about what to expect," he says. "Sid was my mate. A very, very close mate. He just used to laugh at everything; a genius in that way. We did lots of mad things together. We used to busk together. Me with a violin, Sid with a tambourine, maybe a broken guitar!...

"I didn't want him to be a junkie: this is why we travelled on the tour bus together, this is why Sid was to stick with me. He was far too young for that shit... I feel nothing but grief, sorrow and sadness for Sid, to the point that if I really talk about it, I just burst into tears. He was someone I really cared for. I can't be more honest than that. I've lost my friend. I couldn't have changed it. I was too young. God, I wish I was smarter. You can look back on it and think, 'I could have done something'. He died, for fuck's sake! And they just turned it into making money. How hilarious for them. Fucking cheek. I'll hate them forever for doing that. You can't get more evil than that, can you, you know? No respect... Vicious? Poor sod."

Even Glen Matlock, who might have cause to look unkindly on the man who took his place in the Pistols, said soberly: "Sid basically was a... loveable idiot. He looked good and there was a proper band and then there was a media exercise that was him. He swallowed that whole rock 'n' roll lifestyle."

As a performing and recording unit the Sex Pistols were done for—at least until the 1990s—but before Vicious' death, a short-lived incarnation of the Pistols with Ed Tudor-Pole was suggested. As Tudor-Pole told it, "I was just some kid from nowhere and suddenly had McLaren and Bernie Rhodes coming down my squat, then Steve. Steve and I went out for an Indian meal. I was pretty shy of these guys. Then I met Paul. They were very nice chaps, Steve and Paul. Then we rehearsed as a band with a stand-in bass player called Andy Allen... Steve can't half play guitar.

"I was on cloud nine, I didn't know what had hit me. I thought, 'I want to contribute to this band. I can write songs.' I did write songs, [though] I wouldn't call them punk. I wrote a song called 'What's In A Word' for Steve and Paul, but I was a bit of a new boy, so I didn't want to start shoving my own songs in the Sex Pistols' faces on the second rehearsal! We had five rehearsals. But I did show them the song—they said, 'Oh yeah, that's good' and then we went on to something else."

Events moved quickly for Tudor-Pole. "As far as I was concerned I'd got the job. I was now the new singer of the Sex Pistols. And then on the advert for 'Who Killed Bambi?', which was rush-released, it said 'Introducing Ten Pole Tudor.' My heart was in my mouth. In a way I didn't want to be the second Johnny Rotten. I thought, I can't compete with Johnny Rotten, but I wasn't going to get off the train, I was going to see where it led. It would obviously lead somewhere exciting. When it all ended, part of me was relieved because then I could do my own band, and be a band leader myself, which is what I'd always wanted to do."

Nowadays, he looks back on the saga with humor. "I've never managed to live it down. But yeah, it was quite funny. It was all crammed into a very short amount of time, maybe a six-week period. Then Sid Vicious died. McLaren was ousted from control of Glitterbest by a law suit because he'd been squandering all the boys' royalties making the *Rock 'n' Roll Swindle* film, which ate up money. Strictly speaking he shouldn't have spent their money, but McLaren always said you have to speculate to accumulate. So on that technicality they stopped him having anything whatsoever to do with the Sex Pistols, and then Sid died about a day later and the whole thing was finished.

"When Sid died, everything stopped. But I got a bit of money out of the publishing company, Warners, for 'Who Killed Bambi?'. That was recorded very late—it was rushed onto the album. Then the *Swindle* album was released. McLaren said the album was coming out in about two weeks, and 'by the way I'm not calling you Ten Tudor-Pole, I'm calling you Ten Pole Tudor.' I said: 'I'm not sure I like that, really.' He said: 'That's too bad, you're printed on 10,000 copies!'"

After forming a short-lived band called The Professionals with Paul Cook, Steve Jones went on to a fairly low-profile career as a hired gun until the early 1990s, when he joined a band called the Neurotic Outsiders alongside John Taylor of Duran Duran, and Matt Sorum and Duff McKagan of Guns N'Roses. They played a few gigs at the Los Angeles club the Viper Room, but never really made much of themselves. Jones enjoyed the limelight once more in 1996 and 2003, however, when the Sex Pistols reformed and toured to much derision from the press and nostalgic delight from the ageing fanbase. He also launched an internet radio show which has brought him a lot of attention, as well as producing a few rock bands.

Later on Steve played with Ed Tudor-Pole's band. As the latter recalled, "What happened was that Steve didn't know quite what to do with himself. He'd tried The Professionals, but that wasn't exactly full-on. I'd got my band together—no one had really heard of us, but we were beginning to build up a following and Steve used to come along. There wouldn't be that many people there, such as [at] the Moonlight Club in West Hampstead, and he'd come on stage and play on a song or two. He'd often be quite pissed. Once he got up one song too early and just sat on the amp until it was finished, until his turn. We all enjoyed it, it was all good fun. It wasn't like the Second Coming or something, but as time goes on you look at past events and they take on a pattern of glory and glamor which at the time, one's unaware of. It's the reason I'm still going today."

Paul Cook did very little after the demise of The Professionals until the Pistols reunion, other than spots with The Chiefs Of Relief and Edwyn Collins.

Glen Matlock established a low-key but successful career with his own band, who issued a series of Small Faces/Kinks-influenced albums for various labels to critical approval. An early project was The Rich Kids, which also featured Midge Ure, Steve New and Rusty Egan. Matlock also asked Paul Weller to join the band at one stage, as Weller recalled. "I'm not going to join anyone's band, you know—I've got my own band... There was also a time when we asked Glen to join us. That fell through, but after Glen left the Pistols we were talking about him joining and playing guitar, but it wouldn't really have worked out, and we were both nervous so we just left it at that."

Of his time with the Pistols, Matlock later recalled: "There was a lot of stuff going down in England at the time. We didn't set out to be deliberately outrageous: we were just pretty forthright. These days... it's just outrage for outrage. Just before the Pistols, or just after, there was the band The Plasmatics came out, blowing everything up on stage and chainsaws. But they didn't have anything to say—that was what was hollow. We were totally different from that. People don't talk about you 25 years on if you hadn't done something right the first time around."

The Pistols' 1996 reunion tour took a lot of people by surprise. As Matlock, summoned from relative obscurity to fill the role which Sid Vicious had taken from him, recalled: "We did the world tour in 1996, and I wouldn't say [Lydon and I] were best of mates, but acquaintances, yes. I think Paul fell out with him or he fell out with Paul that time. He's a funny kettle of fish, John. What makes Johnny Rotten great as a frontman doesn't necessarily make him great as a person. But then some people like him one way, some people like him the other, and I'm sure he says the same about me anyway."

The tour itself was "what they call a nice little earner," said Matlock with a grin. "Bands that've been going ever since The Clash, they get to play all those good songs for 20 years and we never done that. We had a brief spell and then those songs never got played. When we played live in 1996, most reports were pretty good. There was a couple that slagged us off, of course: it was never going to be exactly the same as the birth of punk. But there was a musical side to the Pistols as well as all the aggro. In Finsbury Park that year we had 12,000 people."

The only Pistol who really succeeded was John Lydon, taking a brave step into a new band—Public Image Ltd—in 1978 with little money and few friends in the industry other than the Virgin execs who had signed him. One of the first things that Lydon did after leaving the Pistols was to visit the Caribbean with his friend Don Letts. While there he opened his mind to a new music scene: that of reggae and dub. His mind was ready for such an experience, as those of all thinking people are to new influences.

As Letts recalled: "John already had that spaciousness, that blueprint in his mind long before we went to Jamaica. As long as I knew John, he had always listened to sparse avant-garde music, stuff like Can, and he really knew his reggae. I have to emphasize that him and Joe Strummer, Paul Simonon, Jah Wobble—they understood dub deeply.

"We went to a lot of sound system sessions here in London too, people like Jah Shaka, Coxsone [Dodd], Moa Anbessa, so really his experiences in Jamaica were an extension of what had already been in his mind for years, back in north London. Isn't that just so obvious when you listen to those early PiL tunes, the stuff he was making with Wobble and Keith [Levene] just after he left the Pistols?"

It is indeed. Little wonder that Lydon's early music with PiL was so eager to explore open spaces: he had loved his time in Jamaica. Letts: "You know, sometimes me and John just had to pinch ourselves to remind ourselves that we weren't dreaming all this! It was great for us to be meeting and working with these guys, guys whose music we really admired and loved."

The admiration worked both ways. "The rastas loved John! To them he was 'the punk rock don from London'—they were aware of all the trouble he had stirred up in London, and yeah, they were into what he stood for and his stance, and they dug it... We smoked a chalice together with U-Roy for breakfast, and then went out to one of his dances, miles out in the countryside. I remember the dreads stringing up this sound, and kicking off with some earthquake dubs. Now let me tell you this sound system was loud, and me and John, both of us, literally passed out! I remember hours later some dreads shaking us awake: it was like, 'Wake up man, dance done, dance finish now man!' Yeah, it was pretty wild out in Jamaica. John just had a vibe you know—people were drawn to him. It was the same in London; it was the same in Kingston."

There is, Letts surmises, a deeper link: "John is Irish, and there is a definite affinity between Jamaicans and Irish. We've all heard the saying 'no Irish, no blacks, no dogs,' which used to appear in pub and lodging windows and well, there must have been a reason for that, that ethnic grouping together, that ethnic rejection... Jamaicans and Irish people have always got on together in England, though I can't say for sure why. A similar attitude to life, perhaps? Who knows why they should tune in to each other's psyches so well... Is it that both are oppressed peoples, or that both have a natural rebelliousness of spirit?"

Hooking up with Keith Levene, a guitarist in an early incarnation of The Clash, plus bassist Jah Wobble (so nicknamed after his real name, John Wordle, was mispronounced) and drummer Jim Walker, Lydon took his experiences with Letts to the recording studio. Taking a step away from any obvious punk sound, the early PiL work was bass-heavy rock with industrial and dub elements overlaid with Lydon's vocals, which he had expanded away from the old sarcastic ranting style of old.

After the unusually catchy debut single 'Public Image' (which reached the Top 10), a self-titled debut album and a second, the more ambitious *Metal Box* (released as three 12-inch discs in a film container), Lydon enjoyed a wave of critical success once again. This time, however, there were far fewer of the establishment-baiting soundbites that had both made and broken the Pistols. Always a shrewd operator, Lydon used PiL as a way into the press and public, disseminating his political and cultural views with more subtlety. Johnny Rotten had grown up, it seemed.

After endless line-up changes and 1980s hits with the 'Rise' single and its accompanying album (the very Situationist *Album*—or *Cassette* or *Compact Disc*, depending on the format you bought), the PiL industry peaked and in 1993 Lydon went solo. The Pistols reunions in 1996 and 2003 kept him in the public eye, as did a fresh round of interviews he conducted for the 2005 Rotten/Lydon best-of compilation *The Best Of British £1 Notes* CD and DVD. This featured work from the Pistols, PiL and his solo work as well as collaborations such as the 'Open Up' single he had recorded with techno act Leftfield in 1993.

Lydon's frank autobiography, *Rotten: No Irish, No Blacks, No Dogs*, detailed his extraordinary life so far in 1994. It's quite a read, and recommended to anyone who enjoys this era in British social history. At one point in the book, Don Letts recalls: "I thought the punks were just a bunch of crazy white people. I didn't really tune into it. When I became the DJ at The Roxy and started meeting them, I picked up on what they were doing... They liked me because I gave them access to Jamaican culture, and they turned me on to a culture that didn't fucking exist before they came along...

"John Lydon was a serious dude because there were very few people around during those times who gave off that aura. I started taking him to reggae clubs. We went to a place called The Four Aces in Dalston, which is the heaviest reggae club in London. No white people went in there. The only white person in there was John, because I took him. Everybody left John alone. We black people had a respect for him because he came across as a real dude. He wasn't created by the media. He could walk into places white people could never go with total immunity... We all felt like society's outlaws."

Lydon wrote of Letts: "Don and I first said hello and hung out after a Pistols gig at The Nashville. We went back to Forest Hill and spent the whole night rapping on about reggae... Don didn't know, but it was the night I was frustrated and getting ready to quit the Pistols. Going to those reggae clubs gave me a lift."

Lydon has also developed a promising multimedia career, moving into TV presenting—he hosted a short-lived VH-1 show called *Rotten TV*—and various documentaries, including a Belgian series called *What Makes Britain Great?* But a rather more significant emergence into the public arena came with 2004's *I'm A Celebrity, Get Me Out Of Here!*, a so-bad-it's-good reality TV show in which 10 lesser media lights (often those who are truly naff or whose 15 minutes are deemed to have passed) are left in an Australian bush camp with little food or shelter. Entertainment comes from the awful tasks which the contestants are required to perform—eating insects, swimming in mucus and so on—while the viewing public enjoys a thrill of power by voting them out one by one.

On this particular series Lydon was the undoubted star, urging the others to combine in order to defeat the aims of the programme makers. However, this failed and he stalked off the set halfway through after calling the viewers 'fucking cunts' on a prime-time show. ITV and the regulating company received 91 complaints: it's doubtful that any irate truckers put their boots through their TV screens this time around.

Of Lydon's later activities, The Clash's Paul Simonon said: "I thought it was brave to jump in at the deep end after the Pistols, but that's John—he doesn't do things by half measures. He's always been very clear on where he's going. A lot of people slagged him off for doing the TV thing but I thought it was good to do because people have the wrong idea of him—like some sort of fat, bean-slurping idiot like in that Alex Cox film *Sid & Nancy*. That pissed me off, making him look like an idiot. Whereas when he did the TV show, the rest of the world saw a very sharp, intelligent human being and that surprised a lot of people. They expected him to be a mindless idiot, but John has a fantastic wit, a wicked sense of humor."

As Lydon, the brain at the front and the back of it all, approached his half-century, he observed philosophically: "This is a difficult life I've got myself into. It's narrow and it's insular, and it becomes very precious sometimes. Sometimes I see myself as slightly too big-headed, but I am trying, and all I ask for people is try too. If you've got something you do and it's better than the way I do what I do, then question me. But until you've actually made a commitment to the human race, shut the fuck up."

Malcolm McLaren, as you might expect, continued with various activities after the Pistols variously left his care. As the flame of the first wave of punk flickered and went out after the band's collapse, he moved on to the New Romantic scene. He is sometimes credited with launching Culture Club and its charismatic lead singer Boy George to stardom (although when I mentioned this to George in 2001, he replied that McLaren was a "shark"—and more pithily, a "cheeky fucking cunt").

What is not in doubt is that McLaren assembled and managed the slightly controversial pop band Bow Wow Wow, who caused some media frothing with one of their record sleeves, which depicted their allegedly then-underage singer Annabella Lwin naked (if discreetly so). He also tried to create more controversy by getting the band to advocate home-taping with cassettes. The industry stirred uneasily but the campaign failed to catch fire and the moment passed.

To many people's surprise, he then enjoyed a brief burst of stardom as a solo performer in his own right, scoring several chart hits between 1982 and 1984. One of these, 'Double Dutch,' even made number 13 in the UK with its infectious gospel/hip-hop mix. Further singles made the UK Top 100 in 1989 and sporadically through the 1990s. In 1991 he wrote and produced a musical called *The Ghosts Of Oxford Street*, which did reasonably well in London theatres, but he failed to achieve any recognition in 1998 with a Spice Girls-alike band called Jungk. A frankly unnecessary remix by Roger Sanchez of his 1982 hit 'Buffalo Gals' came and went the following year.

McLaren remains a figure of note in the British arts establishment—although he would strongly revile the term, no doubt—and it was even speculated that he would stand for London mayor in 2000. However, as Glen Matlock said of the mayoral non-event: "When he tried to become mayor he had to get 10 people from each borough to nominate him. Thing about Malcolm is that he knows about a thousand people in Soho and Bloomsbury, but doesn't know one person in Enfield or Clapton. I heard him interviewed on the radio, all about what he'd do on transport issues, the tube. Malcolm said, 'I don't know, dear man. I always walk everywhere.' I mean, what's he going to have in common with your average man in the street?"

Ed Tudor-Pole, however, remains a committed supporter of McLaren. "He's an amazing man, a one-off buccaneering, maverick, mad, crazed, madman. He's great. Malcolm can say what he likes, he's quite a man in his own right. He's very irreverent, sending people up. There should be more people like him. People are too similar these days."

Perhaps the man who emerged from *The Great Rock 'n' Roll Swindle* with most dignity—apart from Lydon, who had scorned it in the first place—was Julien Temple, who has since forged a respected career as a video and film director. His first post-*Swindle* achievement of note came in 1984 with *Absolute Beginners*, a Britpop film (before the term was coined) that celebrated a technicolor age of Swinging London that never really existed. It starred Patsy Kensit (then a novice actress in a dismal band called Eighth Wonder) and David Bowie, who provided the excellent theme tune. British critics savaged the movie, but American audiences took to it with much more gusto and Temple crossed the Atlantic in 1989 to make the Jim Carrey comedy *Earth Girls Are Easy*. A 1995 thriller, *Bullet*, followed, as did *Vigo: Passion For Life* (1999) and *Pandaemonium* (2000), the story of the friendship between the poets Samuel Coleridge and William Wordsworth.

Temple has also made a name as a music video director, creating promos for Tom Petty, Van Halen, Culture Club, Accept, Whitney Houston and others. "I tried to make mischief on MTV as much as I could," he said. "In the beginning of MTV you could get away with stuff they wouldn't let you do now… Back then you didn't have to rely on a style to get work. I can't think of anything worse than doing the same thing twice. Even though I've made two films about the same subject, I didn't do it in the same way. I don't like videos where you can tell who the director is. I like to try to find out what is unique about that band and why that band means something good or bad and nail that, rather than design a perfume.

"The thing that was attractive to me personally about videos in the beginning was that it was uncharted territory, and in a sense the record companies didn't know what they were doing. So you could continue to play around with ideas that were not necessarily mainstream. I would try to have a sense of humor and an independence with video making, rather than flattering teddy bears or whatever, like a lot of these videos do."

Some of the artists for whom Temple shot videos were aware of his past. "Eric B and Rakim, when I worked with them, they were very aware of the Sex Pistols. Tupac Shakur and Neil Young were. It depends who they are. Janet Jackson is obviously quite an isolated case, as is Whitney Houston. But I think they were aware of my fondness for Hollywood musicals of the 1950s. When I worked with Janet Jackson, I learned that she and Michael used to dance in front of the screen to *Absolute Beginners* in their mansion together, which is a funny idea for me."

Early in the 1990s Lydon, Jones, Cook, Matlock, and the estate of Sid Vicious (collectively Sex Pistols Residuals) won a court case against Malcolm McLaren. One of the results was that *The Great Rock 'n' Roll Swindle* was released on VHS in 1993 and, finally, on DVD 12 years later.

Asked in 2005 how he felt that the *Swindle* was now out on DVD after so long, Temple mused: "We made the DVD a long time ago, so it was ready and waiting for someone to finally put it out. It had a weird history of not being released in the United States so it became an underground thing with terrible quality bootlegs... [Doing the DVD commentary] was weird because you're trying to remember what happened 30 years ago. So it comes in spurts, then something triggers a whole load of things but you don't have time to say them because they want you to do it in real time. I've done it for all the other movies that have come out on DVD but this is the first time I tried to remember conversations I had in a room 25 years ago."

"I was always very fond of that time," added Temple. "But actually doing the film and getting into it again was very energizing. I think you have to take on, to an extent, the personality of the film you're making while you're making it. It did affect me... I've tried to stay true, in my own fashion, to the ideas of the Sex Pistols, even while I was working with bands like Duran Duran or the Stones, whoever it might be."

But Temple remained best known for his work on the Sex Pistols, and the big directing break he needed to make the jump into the big league always seemed to elude him. Perhaps aware of this, he returned to the subject of the Pistols in 2000 when he directed *The Filth And The Fury*. This was a re-telling of the Sex Pistols' tale but with far more sympathy towards the band members and a balanced narrative that took into account the various sides of the story. *"The Filth And The Fury* was the film I owed the Sex Pistols," he said in the director's commentary to the 2005 edition of the *Swindle*.

Asked why he had returned to the subject, Temple explained: "Well, there are a lot of reasons. One, I guess we had spoken about it for a while—the band and myself— because we always knew there was interesting footage that hadn't been used... It's a strange project to do, in a sense, because it's very mad to make a film about the same subject in a way. Particularly about a rock band; I don't think I would do that about any other band. But you weigh those things, and things you're not meant to do are often the best things to do, you know?

"I always felt there was kind of a millennial aspect to the Sex Pistols. It does seem a particularly good time to do it, partly because no one has actually gone further than the Sex Pistols, I don't think, in that cultural music arena. They still challenge people... we found out when we tested the film in England [that] a lot of the younger kids thought it was a fictional piece, beyond *Spinal Tap*. They thought it was actors playing the part of deranged rock stars, or whatever they thought they were. And I think in that context, when a generation of kids is that ignorant of their recent history, it does a good job of showing what the Pistols were standing for.

"It's current and it's in the air," he went on, "partly because I think nothing contemporary is as extreme or as strongly stated as what the Sex Pistols were able to do in their time, in the 1970s. I think the reason to [make the movie] is that their ideas are still alive: the defence of the right to be an individual, and questioning everything you read, and questioning all the information that's bombarded increasingly at you. It's more important than ever, with the opening of the floodgates of information from every corner, to stand up and say that the most important thing about us all is the fact that we're all individuals who can think for ourselves. It's a very defiant cry that's worth paying more and more attention to."

Of McLaren, Temple remarked that he "was involved to the extent that we used taped interviews, but it was very much the band's version of what it was like to go through that process, which in a sense is like a firestorm they went through. It's meant to be a lot more of a human film than the kind of Godardian *Rock 'n' Roll Swindle*. It's more about the reality as it appeared to the people who were actually in that band.

"I see it more as a complementary addition to the whole canon of Sex Pistols-obsessional material, in a way… this is the band's take. It was always a joint project between myself and the band, so I was aware of trying to convey, in my own way, their side of the story and their feelings. So I think that once that was established, I was quite free to do what I wanted, and I did. They never made me change anything, actually."

Asked about the differences between the *Swindle* and *Filth*, Temple explained: "It was just doing it in another way. *Swindle* was designed at a very specific time in a very punk line of approach to blow away some of the rock 'n' roll secretions that accumulated around the Pistols. *The Filth And The Fury* was to tell a much more human story, with 20 years of perspective on what the Sex Pistols and punk had done in terms of changing people's consciousness.

"We also cannibalized some of the *Swindle* to make *The Filth And The Fury* which seemed appropriate… *Swindle* is very much a documentary of its time and was made in the heat of the moment… No one has come up with anything more modern than [the Pistols]. I don't think you can live without that punk feeling. I think the Sex Pistols were just one manifestation of ideas that are constantly around and bubbling under. People have to find new ways of expressing themselves rather recycling the punk look. But I think the attitude is just as modern as it ever was and just as important."

After two decades, it might be expected that Temple would have honed his craft a little. Of *The Filth And The Fury*'s directorial style, he explained: "I see this film as a movie, not as a documentary... I don't know what the conventions are, really. It's certainly not a television-styled documentary. The editing style goes way back to when we used to make films before the Pistols. When they were banned, we would film stuff off television and re-edit TV shows, chop it up, and show films before their gigs. So that cut-up style was very endemic to the ideas of the Pistols, I think. I wanted to get a lot of information across in a short time, as well, so I wanted not to have a linear approach to it. It was very improvized."

But—rather intriguingly—it seems that the old-style approach still held sway to a degree. "We were actually one of the first people to have a video machine in the UK, where you could tape, because we were trying to tape their TV performances, some of which are in the film. The TV companies had [erased] some of them, as well, so the only copies that existed were the ones we taped. Spinning off from that, I would tape lots of movies, and in the movie breaks I would be taping ads and news reports and weather reports. That's really what I mined, and I would come across things and try them out to see how they work.

"It was a very cut-up kind of approach. But I think when you're trying to recapture a sense of time and place, that's quite a good way to do it, because that's the way you experienced living in a place. It's very random. It's not a kind of researched archival quest. Most documentaries have a line, and they find material to fit that line rather than coming across material and seeing how that can change the way you're doing things."

Plus ça change...

Asked how British people's attitude toward the Pistols had changed over the intervening 20 years, Temple pondered: "Twenty years is a long time, so there have been changes throughout that time. There was a sense of them that ties into that group not realizing they were a real band, that no one could be that way because the story is pretty outrageous... There are a lot of bands coming out of the UK now where the only real models are the Sex Pistols, not people like the Stones or the kind of classic rock figures. It's the Sex Pistols, because their attitude is still very modern. They haven't been outstripped. I think there's a great awareness among cutting-edge kids that these people were very important in their time and actually *defined* our time, in some ways.

"I always found it strange when I was making this film that the Pistols came across as very modern contemporary figures, whereas the newscasters and weathermen and chat-show people were kind of monstrous freaks of nature. Obviously, at the time, it was completely the other way around. The Sex Pistols were seen as some mutant virus, and these people were [regarded as] normal.

"Many things have changed in our culture here in England as a direct result of the Pistols. The whole street-fashion thing in London, for example, or the coverage of popular culture in the national press, or the fact that the film industry is now about young people making films about young British issues. All those things are completely different. Even after the 1960s... I think the 1960s had more of a patronising attitude toward youth, or toward young people doing things. But the Pistols blew that away. They said, 'We aren't fucking around, we want to do it now, we're just as good as anyone else, and we have just as much to say as anyone who is older than us.' And that had a big effect on our country.

"I think it did on America [too] in the end. It took longer to come over as a mainstream idea in the States, but I think it's had as big an impact. The main thing I hope is that we can get younger kids as well, so it's not just people who know some of the answers already."

The continuing strength of the Pistols' appeal cannot be denied and the depth of their impact on popular culture is there for all to see, but does the band that once chanted "No future!" still have a future? The band's comeback tour in 2003—again with Glen Matlock on bass—had shaky beginnings, as Lydon revealed beforehand.

"I sort of didn't want to do this tour at first, then I heard Paul Cook didn't... Frankly, it was falling apart, and I thought it was stupid, [but] once our name has been committed to a thing we have to do it, that's just the way I am... Believe me, the original budget was ridiculous, we'd have been seriously out of pocket. So I stepped in and corrected it. Then again, I don't want to say that either, you know what I mean? Because every time I tell the truth of the thing it's seen as I'm being fucking arrogant. I've worked my arse off on this tour."

Asked if he perceived any successors to the Pistols' throne—so to speak; in direct contradiction of everything the *Swindle* set out to achieve—the singer was decisive. "There's no real competition to us. Not that we ever asked for any. I don't see anyone out there really telling it like it is, or showing it like it is. It's quite an outstanding feat for a band that's been around 25-plus years not to have a record label, but that's how ostracized and outside of the industry we are. But hello, fuck it, I'm the living proof [that] we can put a tour together like this without any record company money, and without any need for product. Well, it's self-explanatory—hello, young girls and boys, you too can do this. Fucking ignore the system, use it when it suits you.

"What is punk? It's do it yourself isn't it? And guess what? We're still doing it ourselves. If there's any flags to wave, I honestly don't see anyone out there doing it. They're all so super-starred and structured, and video orientated, it's really negative.

"You can hear the Pistols in a lot of bands, but they won't admit it. They'll rubbish us, and the reason for that is we're the real deal, and they can't come up to that level. We can't play, we can't sing, but you can't say we don't mean a thing."

Would the Pistols continue after these gigs? "I don't know," he replied. "I do not bow to any outside pressure. It's how I feel in my own head, and it's the same with the other three, I hope! I can't speak for them and I wouldn't want to. If we did new songs it would feel gimmicky to me. I'm writing very well on my own right now, and I don't want to clutter all that in with it…

"Oddly, the way the Pistols first started, we were written off as no-hopers, and that freedom gave us an immense chance to just do what we wanted. It's always been that way ever since. I don't have to explain why 'I don't want to' to anybody... I see no reason why we should cease to exist, I really fucking enjoy being on stage with this band, right, but I really enjoy my solo stuff too. I see no reason why the two should be in opposite directions. They are just different things.

"Look, without the Pistols nothing that I do now would be possible, so that's my homage, that's where I learned my trade. Do what I want, be honest to myself and then it would do good for others, that's all, full on."

The tour was preceded in 2002 by a remix of 'God Save The Queen' by Leftfield's Neil Barnes, a slightly weak effort that sounded quaint rather than threatening. Released to coincide with the Queen's Golden Jubilee—how the wheel of history turns!—the song sounded to many like a whisper of "We did it then and we're still here!" from another era.

Lydon still had plenty to say about the Queen, however. "Nobody cares about the monarchy any more, but nobody cares about paying for them either, and that's a curious state of affairs, isn't it? It comes through your tax. You don't care what you're paying your tax money for? It's paying, isn't it, and it isn't your choice. Why don't you have a choice? I don't care if it's a penny a decade, it's not your choice. The royal wave has turned into a royal kiss-off, 'Oh, you dirty things.'

A couple of years years later, he added: "Look—that lot, we laugh at them, we use them, they're pageantry and they somehow bring us all together, and we saucily love 'em. But we don't have to adore them. We don't have to kow-tow to them. As long as we can get over that sense of subservience we're doing all right."

Asked if his band had a future ahead of them, Lydon cackled: "There never was. We never had a future at all. Every day of the Sex Pistols is a miraculous achievement. I can't predict if we will ever meet again, or do anything again. I can't say yes or no, I can't. There's a thing in there that binds us all, and we like it, but I'm not going to become a pantomime about it. There's some serious political things in us that are very important and have to be achieved. If I see that someone else is prepared to take up that gauntlet, I'm more than happy to hand it over, because I've got many other things going on in my life. All of us have other things to do."

Playing with the other band-members was both a spur and a drag, he said. "We genuinely do not like each other as human beings. The way we see things is so different, but when those differences came together it made pure common sense. That natural revulsion we had for each other brought out the best. Because despite the hate it never separated us. We're still attached to each other. There's a common bond there, but none of us can tell you what it is. I'll have a go at them, they'll have a go at me, but if anyone else has a go at them, I'm with them. This is one loyal firm in that respect. No one has earned the right to slag any of them."

His take on the subject was slightly different when he told the author in 2005, "When the Sex Pistols reform every now and again, we do so as mates. Right? Although we probably don't like each other as people, on stage we really like each other. You can't replace that feeling. It gets you in there (*touches chest*), it's a fuckin' amazing reward. So we'll take the bottles and bricks and knives, and we always have, because it's worth it. We've done something valid, for all the pitfalls and stupidities and bickering and bitter remarks. I love those people. I love everyone I've worked with. You should do in life. You should, because there's too little of it. Love is not hippie nonsense, it's something better than that. It's a respect. All these blokes have great integrity, right? They stood there when it mattered... How British is that? We're frontline troops."

Where to end our foul-mouthed story of manipulation and propaganda? Perhaps with the simple premise that *The Great Rock 'n' Roll Swindle*, in attempting to de-iconize the icons it portrayed, did its job so completely that a void was created—a void which needed to be filled, and which has been filled several times over. After all, the cult of celebrity is a more ravenous beast now than it has ever been. The Green Days and Offsprings of this world—and all their teen-friendly, corporate pop-punk colleagues—have a more tenacious grip on the world of popular music than the Pistols ever had.

Maybe the Sex Pistols created more than they destroyed. Maybe their little film, the recorded legacy of their unique presence, shaped the future. Who killed Bambi? We all do—every day. Who got swindled? All of us, of course.

appendix 1

Full Cast and Crew for
The Great Rock 'n' Roll Swindle

Directed by
Julien Temple

Written by
Julien Temple

Cast (in credits order)

Malcolm McLaren	....	The Embezzler
Steve Jones	....	The Crook
Sid Vicious	....	The Gimmick
Paul Cook	....	The Tea-Maker
John Lydon	....	The Collaborator
Mary Millington	....	Mary, The Crook's girlfriend
Irene Handl	....	Cinema Usherette
Edward Tudor-Pole	....	Tadpole (kiosk attendant) (as Eddie Tenpole-Tudor)
Jess Conrad	....	Jess
Liz Fraser	....	Woman in Cinema
Ronald Biggs	....	The Exile (as Ronnie Biggs)
Helen Wellington-Lloyd	....	Helen (as Helen of Troy)
Julian Holloway	....	Man

John Shannon	....	Nazi
Alan Jones	....	Record Executive
Faye Hart	....	Secretary
James Aubrey	....	Record Executive

rest of cast listed alphabetically

Dave Dee	....	Record Executive
James Jeter	....	Martin Boorman
Glen Matlock	....	Ex-Pistol
Sting		
Peter Dean	....	Nightclub Bouncer (uncredited)
Jordan	....	Girl wearing 'anarchists shirt' (uncredited)
Debbie Juvenile	....	Girl on the chorus at the opening track (uncredited)
Nancy Spungen	....	Nancy (uncredited)

Produced by

Don Boyd	....	executive producer
Jeremy Thomas	....	executive producer

Original Music by
Paul Cook (with the Sex Pistols)
Steve Jones (with the Sex Pistols)
John Lydon (with the Sex Pistols)
Ian Samwell (song 'Watcha Gonna Do About It')
Sid Vicious (with the Sex Pistols)

Non-Original Music by
Claude François (song "My Way")

Cinematography by
Adam Barker-Mill (as Adam Barker Mill)
Ku Khanh
Nicholas D. Knowland
John Metcalfe
Willi Patterson

Film Editing by
Richard Bedford
Crispin Green
Mike Maslin
Bernie Pokrzywa
David Rae
Gordon Swire

Costume Design by
Norma Moriceau

Production Management
Joyce Herlihy   ....   production supervisor

Art Department
Celia Barnett   ....   set designer

Sound Department
John Griffiths   ....   sound editor
Brian Paxton   ....   dubbing mixer

| Steve Cook | .... | sound re-recording mixer (uncredited) |

Other crew

Phil Austin	....	animator
Derek W. Hayes	....	animator
Bill Mather	....	animator
Gil Potter	....	animator
Sohie Richmond	....	production coordinator
John Tiberi	....	soundtrack coordinator
Andy Walker	....	animator

appendix 2

Julien Temple Filmography

Glastonbury (2006)

Pandaemonium (2000)

The Filth and the Fury (2000)

Vigo (1998)

Bullet (1996)

Earth Girls Are Easy (1988)

Aria (segment 'Rigoletto') (1987)

Running Out of Luck (1987)

Absolute Beginners (1986)

The Secret Policeman's Private Parts (1984)

Mantrap (1983)

The Secret Policeman's Other Ball (1982)

The Great Rock 'n' Roll Swindle (1980)

Sex Pistols Number 1 (1977)

appendix 3

Some Other Punk Movies Worth Tracking Down

Sid And Nancy (1986) dir. Alex Cox

Rock'n'Roll High School (1979), featuring The Ramones

Jubilee (1978), dir. Derek Jarman, featuring Siouxsie & the Banshees, Wayne County, Adam Ant, plus a meaty acting role for Toyah Willcox

Rude Boy (1980), featuring The Clash

The Punk Rock Movie (1977) dir. Don Letts'

Punk In London (1977). dir. Wolfgang Bild, featuring The Adverts, The Jam, The Killjoys and X-Ray Spex.

Shell Shock Rock (1979), dir. John Davis, documentary on Belfast Punk, featuring SLF, The Parasites, Rudi, The Outcasts and Victim

Born In Flames (1983), dir. Lizzie Borden, featuring Red Crayola and others

D.O.A.: A Right Of Passage (1980), dir. Lech Kowalski featuring the Pistols' tour of the States plus clips of X-Ray

Spex, Generation X and The Rich Kids.

The Offenders' (1980) dir. Beth & Scott B, the New York 'no wave' scene featuring Lydia Lunch & Teenage Jesus, The Contortions, DNA, Lounge Lizards, The Heartbreakers, The Bush Tetras and Judy Nylon

Another State Of Mind (1983) featuring Social Distortion, Youth Brigade, Minor Threat

Desperate Teenage Lovedolls (1984), dir. David Markey, featuring Redd Kross, The Bangles and Black Flag.

Decline Of Western Civilisation (1981), featuring X, Black Flag, The Germs and Circle Jerks

Up In Smoke (1978), featuring Cheech & Chong plus The Dils, The Whores, and the Berlin Brats

1991: The Year That Punk Broke (1991) dir. David Markey, documentary of the American grunge/hardcore invasion, featuring Dinosaur Jr, Babes In Toyland, Nirvana, The Ramones, Gumball and Sonic Youth

Urgh! A Music War (1981), featuring John Cooper-Clarke, Chelsea, Dead Kennedys, Gary Numan, Joan Jett, The Cramps, The Au Pairs, Devo, Pere Ubu, Magazine, Gang Of Four, X and The Police,

Blank Generation (1976) featuring Patti Smith, Television,

Talking Heads, Ramones and Blondie),

Blitzkrieg Bop (1979) featuring Blondie, The Ramones and The Dead Boys

Punking Out (1977), featuring The Dead Boys, Richard Hell, The Ramones and Lydia Lunch), all filmed at CBGB's

Breaking Glass (1980) dir. Brian Gibson, featuring Hazel O'Connor

appendix 4

Sex Pistols timeline

1976

12 February
The Sex Pistols open for Eddie & The Hot Rods at the
Marquee. The *NME* says: "Don't look over your shoulder,
but the Sex Pistols are coming" and refers to their "1960s-
styled white punk rock."

14 February
The Pistols play at Andrew Logan's Valentine's Ball.

20 February
Soon-to-be Buzzcocks Howard Devoto and Pete Shelley go
to High Wycombe in Buckinghamshire to see the Pistols.

30 March
The Pistols play the 100 Club in London.

4 April
The Pistols start a residency at the El Paradiso club in Soho.
Rotten tells Sounds: "I hate hippies and what they stand for.
I hate long hair… I want people to see us and start
something, or else I'm just wasting my time."

11 May

The Pistols begin a Tuesday night residency at the 100 Club. Jones sums up their career so far: "We started out doing old Small Faces songs as they were the easiest to play. After two months we played at a university and got thrown off stage. They cut the power after 15 minutes. Then we supported The Roogalators and the guy from the 100 Club on Oxford Street heard us. He offered us a gig once a week at the 100 Club. At first there was just a few in the audience, then more and more came. In the end the place was packed. With a big queue outside."

An early regular at the club is Sid Vicious, whose aggressive jumping causes a new dance tag. As he later told *ZigZag*, "I invented the Pogo especially to knock those people all over the place. That's what it was for, that's what people don't seem to realize. It was meant to be a beastly thing for knocking the Bromley Contingent all over the 100 Club!"

20 May

The band record a session with producer Chris Spedding.

4 June

The famous Manchester Lesser Free Trade Hall show, organized by Devoto and Shelley. Fewer than 100 people turn up, but more than 1,000 will claim to have attended.

4 July

The Clash open for the Pistols at the Black Swan in Sheffield.

6 July
The Damned open for the Pistols at the 100 Club.

13 July
Sniffin' Glue fanzine is launched, edited by former bank
clerk Mark Perry.

18 July
Engineer Dave Goodman records the Pistols in a Denmark
Street rehearsal studio. (Denmark Street is London's
equivalent of Tin Pan Alley.)

29 August
The Pistols, The Clash and Buzzcocks play at the Screen
On The Green in Islington, London.

3 September
The Pistols play Paris with the Bromley Contingent
in attendance.

4 September
The Pistols appear on Granada TV's *So It Goes*.

20 September
The 100 Club Punk Festival takes place over two nights
with The Subway Sect, Siouxsie & The Banshees, The
Clash, the Pistols, The Damned, The Vibrators and
Buzzcocks. *Sounds* and *Melody Maker* publish features
on punk rock.

9 October
The Pistols sign to EMI for £40,000. A spokesman says, "They've got to happen for all our sakes."

10 October
The Pistols enter Lansdowne Studios with producer Dave Goodman.

14 October
Another session with EMI staff producer Mike Thorne.

17 October
The Pistols record at Wessex Studios with Chris Thomas.

19 November
'Anarchy In The UK' is *Sounds'* single of the week.

29 November
The Pistols' show at Lancaster Polytechnic is banned by town authorities.

1 December
Bill Grundy's *Today* show, on which Steve Jones comments "You dirty bastard... You dirty fucker... What a fuckin' rotter!" The TV station is flooded with complaints: one idiot viewer puts his foot through his TV screen in protest.

2 December
Several dates on the 'Anarchy' tour are cancelled after newspaper headlines such as "The Filth And The Fury."

4 December
The Pistols refuse to 'audition' for Derby town councillors, who ban that evening's show in the town.

7 December
EMI chairman Sir John Read tells shareholders, "We shall do everything we can to restrain their public behavior."

1977

4 January
The band leave for a short tour of Holland and, according to the press, "spit, vomit and swear" in the terminal at Heathrow airport.

6 January
EMI terminate the Pistols' contract, order the pressing plants to stop production of the 'Anarchy' single and delete it. As Steve Jones puts it: "The board hated us. John Read has fucking dinner with the Queen. How would he explain us to her? A lot of the people at EMI liked us, but not the board. Stupid. We got lots of money without doing anything."

28 January
EMI agree a financial settlement of £30,000 on top of their advance of £20,000.

13 February
Sid Vicious tells a Los Angeles radio station that he has "auditioned" for the Pistols.

28 February
Glen Matlock leaves the band and is replaced by Vicious.

9 March
The Pistols sign to A&M at the offices of Rondor Music, the company's publishing arm.

10 March
McLaren re-stages the A&M contract signing outside Buckingham Palace for the media.

12 March
The Pistols are involved in a fight at the Speakeasy Club with people including 'Whispering' Bob Harris, presenter of *The Old Grey Whistle Test*. One of the TV show's engineers requires 14 stitches in his head.

16 March
Harris' solicitors send a note to Derek Green, managing director at A&M, who discusses the matter with the label's founders Jerry Moss and Herb Alpert. The decision is made to cancel the Pistols' contract and halt production of 'God Save The Queen.' Some copies make it to the public and in 2006 are worth £5,000-£6,000.

28 March
The Pistols play Leicester Square's Notre Dame Hall, owned by the Roman Catholic church. NBC film it for a documentary. The punk movement is in full swing, and the Pistols have many imitators, to Lydon's chagrin: "I get very

sick with the imitations. I despise them. They ruin it. They have no reason to be in it other than wanting money, which shows. You've got to have your own point of view. You can have an idol, like you may see a band and think 'God, that band are really fucking good, I'd like to be like that.' So you start up your own band, and then your own ideas come in as well on top of that and you have a foundation. But a lot of those bands don't leave that foundation, and they stay in a rut and they listen to all the other songs in their morbid little circle and they do rewrites of them. Hence 50,000 songs about how hard it is to be on the dole… You're copying something else, something that comes from inside us and not inside you, and you can't imitate what somebody else is. It doesn't make you a better person, it makes you a worse person. If you're not offering what you are to the world, then I don't want to know. I don't want to hear someone trying to be me, I don't find that impressive."

31 March
The band take a break in Berlin, where they stay at the Hotel Kaplinsky and view the Berlin Wall and other sites.

4 April
The Pistols play a showcase gig at the Screen On The Green with The Slits in support. The Pistols' performance is filmed by Don Letts for his *Punk Rock Movie*.

4 May
LWT's London programme suggests a connection between

the Sex Pistols and the National Front. McLaren refutes
the claim in the *NME*.

12 May
Virgin sign the Pistols. Lydon later reflects: "It's a constant
fucking battle. The Sex Pistols weren't set up with a record
contract from day one, and with Malcolm's bloody phony
showbiz nonsense, we were just about the last punk band to
be signed!"

13 May
Sid is released from hospital after treatment for hepatitis.

17 May
Staff at Virgin's pressing plant initially refuse to make the
pressing plates for 'God Save The Queen.'

18 May
The sleeve artwork plate-makers also initially refuse to
work.

19 May
Thames TV refuse to air an ad for 'God Save The Queen'
during a break in the Bill Grundy show.

23 May
The Pistols book the Marquee to film a live promo for the
new single for *Top Of The Pops*.

27 May
'God Save The Queen' is released with Virgin's biggest advertising campaign to date.

28 May
The *Islington Gazette* runs an interview with Johnny's mother, Eileen Lydon.

31 May
The BBC ban 'God Save The Queen.' The Independent Broadcasting Authority issues a warning to radio stations that the single may be in breach of Section 4:1:A of the Broadcasting Act.

7 June
Virgin and the Pistols celebrate the Queen's Jubilee with the Thames boat trip. There are 11 arrests on its return. Of McLaren's arrest, Lydon later said: "How he squealed, 'It wasn't me—it was them!' And he didn't help anyone out that night. Many people went to jail, and he bailed himself out but he didn't help out any of his so-called friends! Right? Selfish little sod."

18 June
'God Save The Queen' reaches number two without daytime radio airplay. Johnny Rotten, producer Chris Thomas and studio boss Bill Price are attacked outside a London pub. Rotten has his arm slashed and suffers tendon damage.

1 July

Virgin releases the 'Pretty Vacant' / 'No Fun' single.

8 July

Boots' stores agree to stock the new single. McLaren is in
America attempting to set up a tour and raise interest in the
concept of *The Great Rock 'n' Roll Swindle*, under the working
title of *Who Killed Bambi?*

16 July

London's Capital Radio broadcasts a 90-minute show called
A Punk And His Music, on which Johnny plays songs by Tim
Buckley, Neil Young, and Captain Beefheart, among others.

1 August

A bootleg album, *No Fun*, is being sold, taken from the
Dave Goodman EMI sessions.

2 August

Vicious is fined £125 for carrying a knife at the 100 Club
Punk Festival the previous September. He pays the fine and
rejoins the band in Scandinavia.

15 October

'Holidays In The Sun' is released.

28 October

The Sex Pistols' debut album, *Never Mind The Bollocks... Here's
The Sex Pistols* is released. A second bootleg LP, *Spunk*, is
available, featuring original Pistols demos.

1 November

The financial backers of *Who Killed Bambi?* pull out. Director Russ Meyer returns to the US.

5 November

The manager of Virgin's shop in Nottingham is arrested after displaying a poster of the ...*Bollocks* LP cover in the window. Police enforce the 1898 Indecent Advertising Act.

7 November

High-street stores refuse to sell the album and independent shops sell it under the counter. A £40,000 advertising campaign is useless: no one will accept adverts for the LP.

16 November

A major rewrite of the *Swindle* movie script is underway by Pistols film archivist Julien Temple and McLaren.

24 November

Christopher Seale, manager of Virgin's Nottingham shop, is in court. A Professor of English is summoned to explain the history of the word 'bollocks': the case is dismissed and the cover ruled to be 'decent.'

30 November

Vicious gets drunk, goes to his hotel and decides to jump out of the window. His girlfriend Nancy Spungen stops him but he turns on her. Police are called and find an illegal substance: Sid and Nancy are taken to the police station but later released.

9 December

Sid and Nancy split after pressure from the rest of the band to do so. They later resume their relationship.

25 December

The Pistols play a Christmas party at Ivanhoe's Club in Huddersfield for the children of local firemen, laid-off workers and single parents.

29 December

The band have their US entry visas refused because they all have criminal records. Explanations for the convictions are required.

30 December

The visas are issued.

1978

14 January

The Pistols play their last gig at the Winterland Ballroom in San Francisco.

1996

The Pistols reform after 18 years for a series of shows. Lydon later says of the tour: "Loved it! Loved it. Loved the gigs. As people, as a band, we hated each other, but we loved the gigs, and that made perfect sense. It went on a bit because we probably over-committed, but that's the Pistols, we're full-on 100 per cent commitment. We always have been. Our crowd don't care if I'm fat or thin, it's what I'm saying. But music papers, or the middle class, to them it's the image that is essential. The Sex Pistols are not a bunch of clothes-horses, we're not puppets...

"There's a problem about me being seen as arrogant, talking too much, and it's wrong I should feel like that. I've talked too much in the past before I've actually finished a thing, and the idea will be stolen off me. I'm not giving any more out until I've done a thing. I'm fed up with it, I'm fed up with the lack of respect. Respect is the thing I give most people, I'm friendly until it goes the other way."

2002

To tie in with the Queen's Golden Jubilee, a remix of 'God Save The Queen' by Leftfield's Neil Barnes is released. Lydon says: "I always like working with Neil Barnes, and I'm very pleased with the way it came out. That record refers directly to our roots. There's T-Rex indications, there's all kind of stuff. Yet it's simplistic and sing-along childish. There's nothing wrong with that. I love pop music. It's harmless fun, but you can also use fun to educate, to improve..."

2003

The Pistols re-reform for another lucrative tour. Lydon later tells the author: "Thirty thousand of us stuck in a field in Crystal Palace, and we didn't harm each other. That wasn't understood. There were some serious thugs in that field, all mixed up with families and kids, and the riot police at the top of the hills had nothing to do. We beat them. We showed them a lesson."

2006

The 30th anniversary of punk. Asked the previous year if the idea has any legitimacy, Lydon laughs: "No! It's absolutely ridiculous, isn't it? Stop it. What do you think a 30th anniversary of punk show is going to be like? It's going to be full of shammy acts, isn't it? A bitter hissy fest of jealousies and paranoias. These blokes and girls had no sense of unity. Most of them were just copying. Hanging on to the shirt-tails of something else."

appendix 5

UK singles discography

Date	Title	Label / No.

Nov. 1976   Anarchy In The UK / I Wanna Be Me
(5,000 in plain black sleeve with Chris Thomas production credit on B-side.)
EMI / EMI 2566

Nov. 1976   Anarchy In The UK / I Wanna Be Me
(Company sleeve with Dave Goodman production credit on B-side.)
EMI / EMI 2566

March 1977   God Save The Queen / No Feelings
(withdrawn, no picture sleeve.)
A&M / AMS 7284

May 1977   God Save The Queen / Did You No Wrong
Virgin / VS 181

July 1977   Pretty Vacant / No Fun
Virgin / VS 184

Oct. 1977   Holidays In The Sun / Satellite
Virgin / VS 191

Dec. 1977   Lentilmas—A Seasonal Offering To You
From Virgin Records (*Christmas freebie
flexi-disc, some with Christmas card.*)

Lyntone / LYN 3261

June 1978   No One Is Innocent (A Punk Prayer By
Ronald Biggs) / My Way

Virgin / VS 220

June 1978   The Biggest Blow (A Punk Prayer By
Ronald Biggs) / My Way
12 inch.

Virgin / VS 22012

June 1978   The Biggest Blow (A Punk Prayer by
Ronald Biggs) /Interview / My Way
12 inch.

Virgin / VS 22112

Feb. 1979   Something Else / Friggin' In The Riggin'
(*Some copies issued with colour labels,
others with black and white.*)

Virgin / VS 240

March 1979   Silly Thing / Who Killed Bambi?

Virgin / VS 256

June 1979   C'mon Everybody / God Save The Queen
Symphony / Watcha Gonna Do About It?

Virgin / VS 272

| Oct. 1979 | The Great Rock 'n' Roll Swindle / Rock Around The Clock (w/Tenpole Tudor) *'American Express' picture sleeve.* |
| | Virgin / VS 290 |

Oct. 1979   The Great Rock 'n' Roll Swindle / Rock
Around The Clock (w/lawyers' telephone
conversation) *'American Express' picture sleeve.*
Virgin / VS 290

June 1980   (I'm Not Your) Steppin' Stone / Pistols
Propaganda
Virgin / VS 339

Dec. 1980   Pistols Pack. (6 x 45s in 'accordion' plastic
wallet: God Save The Queen / Pretty Vacant;
Holidays In The Sun / My Way; Something
Else / Silly Thing; Steppin' Stone/Anarchy
In The UK; Black Leather / Here We Go
Again; C'mon Everybody / The Great
Rock 'n' Roll Swindle
Virgin / SEX 1

Sept. 1981   Who Killed Bambi? / Rock Around The
Clock (both credited to Tenpole Tudor with
the Sex Pistols)
Virgin / VS 443

1983   Anarchy In The UK/No Fun
Virgin / VS 609

1983   Anarchy In The UK / No Fun / EMI
                12 inch.

                                    Virgin / VS 609-12

Oct. 1984   Interview
                12 inch picture disc.

                                        Pig Dog / PD 1

1985   Anarchy In The UK / EMI / No Fun
                3 inch CD.

                                    Virgin / CDT 3

1985   Submision / No Feelings
                5,000 only. Blue, pink or yellow vinyl.
                Chaos / DICK 1

1985   Submission / Anarchy In The UK
                12 inch. Pink or yellow vinyl.

                                Chaos / EXPORT 1

1986   Anarchy In The U. (Live) / Flogging A
                Dead Horse
                12 inch.

                                        JOCK 120

Aug. 1986   The Original Sex Pistols Live
                (Anarchy In The UK / I'm A Lazy Sod /
                Pretty Vacant /Substitute)
                12 inch, limited to 5,000 copies.

                                Archive 4 / TOF 104

Oct. 1988	The Original Pistols (Anarchy In The UK / Pretty Vacant / No Fun / Substitute [all live]) CD.	
		CDEP 13C

Oct. 1988	Cash For Chaos (Submission [live] /God Save The Oueen / Liar)	
		SPCFC 102

Dec. 1988	God Save The Queen / Did You No Wrong / Don't Give Me No Lip Child *3 inch CD.*	
		Virgin / CDT 37

1988	Pretty Vacant / I Wanna Be Me *(free with* Spiral Scratch *magazine, issue 4). B-side plays 'Seventeen'.*	
		Scratch 4

1990	The Early Years Live (Anarchy In The UK / Pretty Vacant / Liar / Dolls (aka New York) [all live]) *12 inch, blue vinyl.*	
		Replay 3012

Sept. 1992	Anarchy In The UK / I Wanna Be Me	
		Virgin / VS 1431

Sept. 1992   Anarchy In The UK / I Wanna Be Me
               Cassingle.

                              Virgin / VSC 1431

Sept. 1992   Anarchy In The UK (demo version) /
               I Wanna Be Me
               CD.

                              Virgin / VSCDT 1431

Sept. 1992   Anarchy In The UK / Anarchy In The
               UK(demo version) / I Wanna Be Me
               CD with poster.

                              Virgin / VSCDX 1431

Nov. 1992   Pretty Vacant / No Feelings

                              Virgin / VS 1448

Nov. 1992   Pretty Vacant / No Feelings (demo version) /
               Satellite (demo version) / Submission
               (demo no.1)
               12 inch.

                              Virgin / VST 1448

Nov. 1992   Pretty Vacant / No Feelings (demo version) /
               EMI (Unlimited Edition) demo version) /
               Satellite (demo version)
               CD in digipack with space for next CD.

                              Virgin / VSCDG 1448

June 1996   Pretty Vacant [live] / Buddies aka Bodies
              Virgin / VUS 113

June 1996   Pretty Vacant [live] / Buddies aka Bodies /
         No Fun / Problems (Spedding demo)
              Virgin / VUSCD 113

May 2002   God Save the Queen (original version) /
         Neil Barnes [Leftfield] & the Sex Pistols
         7-inch extended mix
              Virgin / VS 1832

May 2002   God Save The Queen (original version) /
         Neil Barnes [Leftfield] & the Sex Pistols
         dance mix / Neil Barnes [Leftfield] & the
         Sex Pistols 7-inch extended mix
         12 inch / CD single
            Virgin / VST / VSDT 1832

appendix 6

Selected albums discography

Date	Title	Label / No.
Oct. 1977	Never Mind The Bollocks… Here's The Sex Pistols	Virgin / V 2086

Holidays in the Sun / Bodies / No Feelings / Liar / God Save the Queen / Problems / Seventeen / Anarchy In The UK / Submission / Pretty Vacant / New York / EMI

| Feb. 1979 | The Great Rock 'n' Roll Swindle | Virgin / VD 2510 |

God Save the Queen [Symphony] / Rock Around The Clock / Johnny B. Goode / Road Runner / Black Arabs / Anarchy In The UK / Whatcha Gonna Do About It? / Who Killed Bambi? / Silly Thing / Substitute / Don't Give Me No Lip Child / (I'm Not Your) Steppin' Stone / Lonely Boy / Something Else / Anarchie Pour Le UK / Belsen Was A Gas / Einmal War Belsen Wirflich Bortrefflich / No One Is Innocent / My Way / C'mon

Everybody / EMI (Orch) / Great Rock 'n' Roll
Swindle / You Need Hands / Friggin' In The
Riggin'

July 1979   Some Product—Carri On Sex Pistols
Virgin / VR 2

Very Name Sex Pistols / From Beyond The
Grave / Big Tits Across America / Complex
World Of Johnny Rotten / Sex Pistols Will
Play / Is The Queen A Moron / Fucking
Rotter

Oct. 1992   Kiss This
Virgin / V 2702

Anarchy In The UK / God Save The Queen /
Pretty Vacant / Holidays In The Sun /
I Wanna Be Me / Did You No Wrong /
Satellite / Don't Give Me No Lip Child /
Stepping Stone / Bodies / No Feelings /
Liar / Problems / Seventeen / Submission /
EMI / My Way / Silly Thing

June 1996   Never Mind The Bollocks / Spunk
(aka This is Crap)
Virgin SPUNK 1

Disc 1 (NMTB): Holidays In The Sun /
Bodies / No Feelings / Liar / God Save The

Queen / Problems / Seventeen / Anarchy In The UK / Submission / Pretty Vacant / New York / EMI

Disc 2 (Spunk / This is Crap): Seventeen / Satellite / Feelings (No Feelings) / Just Me (I Wanna Be Me) / Submission / Nookie (Anarchy In The UK) / No Future (GSTQ) / Problems / Lots Of Fun (Pretty Vacant) / Liar / Who Was That (EMI) / Looking For A Kiss (New York) / Problems / No Feelings / Pretty Vacant / Submission / No Feelings / EMI / Satellite / Seventeen / Anarchy In The UK

July 1996   Filthy Lucre Live

Virgin / CDVUS 116

Bodies / Seventeen / New York / No Feelings / Did You No Wrong / God Save The Queen / Liar / Satellite / (I'm Not Your) Steppin' Stone / Holidays In The Sun / Submission / Pretty Vacant / EMI / Anarchy In The UK / Problems

May 2000   The Filth And The Fury

Virgin / CDVD 2909

Disc 1: God Save the Queen [Symphony] / Shang-A-Lang - Bay City Rollers / Pictures Of Lily - The Who / Virginia Plain - Roxy

Music / School's Out - Alice Cooper /
Skinhead Moonstomp - Simaryp / Glass Of
Champagne - Sailor / Through My Eyes -
The Creation / Jean Genie - David Bowie /
I'm Eighteen - Alice Cooper / Submission /
Don't Give Me No Lip Child / What'cha
Gonna Do About It / Road Runner /
Substitute / Seventeen

Disc 2: Anarchy In The UK / Pretty Vacant /
Did You No Wrong / Liar / EMI / No
Feelings / I Wanna Be Me / Way Over (In
Dub) - Tapper Zukie / Looking For A Kiss -
New York Dolls / Holidays In The Sun /
No Fun

June 2002   Jubilee

Virgin / CDV 2961

God Save the Queen / Anarchy In The UK /
Pretty Vacant / Holidays In The Sun /
No One Is Innocent / My Way / Something
Else / Friggin' in the Riggin' / Silly Thing /
C'mon Everybody / The Great Rock 'n' Roll
Swindle / (I'm Not Your) Steppin' Stone /
Pretty Vacant [Live] / EMI (Unlimited
Edition)

2002   CD ROM:
God Save the Queen [promo video] /

Anarchy In The UK [promo video] /
Pretty Vacant [promo video]
Singles compilation issued to celebrate the Sex Pistols'
25th Anniversary Jubilee. Spans from 'Anarchy In
The UK', through the 'The Great Rock 'n' Roll
Swindle' era to 'Pretty Vacant [Live]' in 1996.

June 2002   Sex Pistols Box Set
                              Virgin Records / SEXBOX1

Disc 1: Studio Tracks & Early Demos
Never Mind The Bollocks... Here's The Sex Pistols
Original Analogue Master:
Holidays In The Sun / Bodies / No Feelings /
Liar / God Save The Queen / Problems /
Seventeen / Anarchy In The UK /
Submission / Pretty Vacant / New York /
EMI (Unlimited Edition) /
B-sides:
I Wanna Be Me / No Feeling (bonus B-side) /
Did You No Wrong / No Fun* (unedited) /
Satellite /
Majestic Studios Demo Session May 1976:
Problems / Pretty Vacant / No Feelings

Disc 2: Demos & Rarities
Denmark Street Demo Session July 1976:
Pretty Vacant / Submission /
Wessex Studios Session October 1976:
Anarchy In The UK /

Wessex Studios Rehearsal Session October 1976:
Substitute / Don't Give Me No Lip Child /
(I'm Not Your) Steppin' Stone / Johnny B.
Goode / Road Runner / Watcha Gonna Do
About It? / Through My Eyes* /
Rejected version of the Anarchy In The UK
7-inch single)
Anarchy In The UK*
Manchester Square Demo Session December 1976*:
No Feelings (instrumental) / No Future /
Liar / Problems /
Gooseberry Studios January 1977:
New York / God Save The Queen /
Wessex Studios Never Mind the Bollocks...
Outtakes May-August 1977:
Satellite / EMI / Seventeen / No Feelings /
Submission (version #1) /

Disc 3 :Live at Screen On The Green '76,
plus live rarities
Islington Screen On The Green cinema, 29 Aug '76*:
Anarchy In The UK / I Wanna Be Me /
Seventeen / New York / (Don't Give Me)
No Lip / (I'm Not Your) Stepping Stone /
Satellite / Submission / Liar / No Feelings /
Substitute / Pretty Vacant / Problems /
Did You No Wrong / No Fun /
London, Nashville Rooms, 3 April '76*
Understanding (live bonus track) /
London, 100 Club, 29 June '76*

Flowers Of Romance #1 (live bonus track) /
Birmingham, Barbarellas, 14 August '76*
Flowers Of Romance #2 (live bonus track) /
Dallas, Longhorns Ballroom, USA, 10 Jan. 78*
Belsen Was A Gas (live bonus track)
* previously unreleased

index

A Hard Day's Night 61, 134
Abba 50
Absolute Beginners 151, 152
Accept 151
Adam & the Ants 15, 68, 135
Adverts, The 45
Allen, Andy 140
Alpert, Herb 46
'Anarchy in The UK' 28, 29, 36
Anbessa, Moa 144
Any Which Way You Can 128
Aubrey, James 107

Bard, Stanley 72
Barnes, Neil 160
Barrett, Syd 38
Bay City Rollers, The 41, 50, 60
Bayley, Roberta 21
Beatles 40, 41, 61
Bedford, Richard 69
Bee Gees, The 54
'Belsen Was A Gas' 51, 113
Beneath The Valley Of the Ultravixens 55
Best of British £1 Notes, The 147
Beverly, Ann 40, 75, 77
Beverly, Simon John 13
Beyond The Valley Of The Dolls 55
Biggs, Ronnie 22–3, 51, 58, 112–13
Black Arabs, The 97, 98, 133
Black Hole, The 128
'Black Leather' 133
Black Stallion, The 128
black youth in London 98–100
Blackburn, Tony 48
Bolan, Marc 61
Boogie 89
Born to Boogie 61
Bow Wow Wow 149
Bowie, David 151
Boy George 149
Boyd, Don 68
Branson, Richard 46–7
Brazil 21, 22–3, 51, 112–13
Bromley Contingent 15–17, 91, 127

Buckingham Palace 40, 101, 135
'Buffalo Gals' 150
Bullet 151
Buñuel, Luis 97
Burns, Jake 130

Chelsea Hotel, New York 70–3
Chiefs of Relief, The 142
Chien Andalou, Un 97
Clash, The 34, 52, 122, 135, 144, 146, 148
Collins, Edwyn 142
Come Play With Me: The Life And Films of Mary Millington 65
Conrad, Jess 67–8
Cook, Paul 15, 21, 22–3, 49, 51, 69, 140, 141, 142
Cooper, Alice 39
County, Jayne 106, 130, 131–3, 136–8
County, Wayne 135
Coxsone [Dodd] 144
Cox, Alex 67, 138, 148–9
Crabs 135
Crossroads television series 68
Crystal Maze television series 67
Culture Club 149, 151

Damned, The 26, 28, 34, 52
de Brett, Tona 93–4
Dean, Peter 97–8
Debord, Guy 61, 100
Division, Joy 39
Doonican, Val 39
Doors, The 40
'Double Dutch' 150
Duran Duran 142, 153

Earth Girls Are Easy 151
Ebert, Roger 55, 56
Egan, Rusty 143
Eighth Wonder 151
'EMI' 133
Empire Strikes Back, The 128
Establishment as the enemy 26–7

F for Fake 128
Faces, The 15, 40, 41
Faithfull, Marianne 63
Faster, Pussycat! Kill! Kill: 55
Festival of Punk Rock 26
Fields, Danny 35
Filth and the Fury, The [film] 129, 139, 153–5
comparison with *The Great Rock 'n'*
Roll Swindle 155–7
Filth and the Fury, The [headline] 31
'First Cut Is The Deepest, The' 49
Four Aces, The 147
Frampton, Peter 46

Genesis 39
Ghosts of Oxford Street, The 150
Gillett, Charlie 48
Glitterbest 53, 141
'God Save The Queen' 46, 47, 61, 81,
130, 160
Godard, Jean-Luc 79, 129, 155
Godspell 67
Goodman, Dave 28
Great Rock 'n' Roll Swindle, The
animation 69, 96, 102
audience mocked by film they
were watching 127
audience reaction 128–9
band members genuinely do
not like each other 161
British institution 8
cast list 163–4
chaotic film-making 62
comparison with *The Filth and the*
Fury 155–7
crew list 163, 164–6
cut-up style endemic to the Sex
Pistols 156–7
DVD release 152–3
end of an era 66–7
enjoyment of others' misfortunes 84
film structure 62
format as ten 'lessons' 79
importance in environment of
the time 134
incoherent structure 7–8
Jubilee 135
Kendon Films 68
Lydon refusal to be involved 58, 68–9
makers wish to alienate fans 59

Marylebone Station 62, 107
McLaren as main character 79
McLaren publicity 63
mischievous joke intention 60
plans for 50–1, 53
public reaction 134
rock 'n' roll reality 136–7
seen as a monster creation 77–8
soundtrack 68, 138
VHS release 152
Warner Brothers finance 56
Great Rock 'n' Roll Swindle, The album 133
Great Rock 'n' Roll Swindle, The missing
features
heroin 123–4
Lydon, John 124–5
Matlock, Glen 117
Never Mind The Bollocks... Here's The
Sex Pistols album 117–19
punk scene violence 122–3
Westwood, Vivienne 119–21
Great Rock 'n' Roll Swindle, The
scenes ['lessons']
0. opening scene 80–1
1. How To Manufacture Your Group
81–8
2. Establish The Name Sex Pistols
88–90
3. Sell the Swindle 90–4
4. Don't Play, Don't Give The
Game Away 94–5
5. Steal Money From The Record
Company Of Your Choice 96–101
6. Become The World's Greatest
Tourist Attraction 102–4
7. Cultivate Hatred 104–7
8. Diversify Your Business 107–8
9. Take Civilisation To The
Barbarians 108–9
10. Who Killed Bambi? 109–16
11. Ending 116–17
Green Day 136, 162
Green, Crispin 69
Green, Derek 36, 46
Grundy, Bill 29–31, 33, 94–5, 121
Guns N'Roses 142

Halen, Van 151
Hammill, Peter 39
Handl, Irene 67, 115

Harris, Bob 'Whispering' 46
Hayes, Derek W 69
Head 134
Heartbreakers, The 24, 34
Hell, Richard 24
'Here We Go Again' 133
hippie movement 12–13
Honky Tonk programme 48
Houston, Whitney 151
Hughes, Rob 69
Hurrah's 76

I Was A Teenage Sex Pistol 30
It's Over 39
I'm A Celebrity Get Me Out Of Here 148
'I'm A Lazy Sod' 25

Jackson, Janet 152
Jamaica 144–5, 147
Jam, The 45
Jarman, Derek 68, 90, 131, 135
Johannesson, Sture 42
Johnny Thunders' Allstars 52
Jones, Steve 14–15, 18, 21, 22–3,
    29, 40–1, 51–2, 62–3, 65, 69,
    127, 140, 141–2
*Joseph And The Amazing Technicolor
    Dreamcoat* 67
Journey 40–1
Jubilee 68, 131, 135–6
Jungk 150

Kensit, Patsy 151
Kilmister, Ian 'Lemmy' 13
Kinks 41
Kramer vs Kramer 128

Lancaster Polytechnic 29
Led Zeppelin 54
Leftfield 160
Leon, Neon 72
Let It Rock [shop] 18
Letts, Don 44–5, 46, 71,
    99–100, 123, 144–8
Levene, Keith 10, 145, 146
Lindsay, John 64
Logan, Andrew 90–1
Loggins, Dan 27
'London Boys' 52
Lucas, Sue 'Catwoman' 88, 107, 127

Lwin, Annabella 149
Lydon, John *[Johnny Rotten]*
    absence from *The Great Rock 'n' Roll
        Swindle* 68–9, 124–5
    anger towards McLaren 10–11
    attacked 49, 102
    attitude to money 53–4
    autobiography 147
    background 9–13
    Bill Grundy show 29–30
    Catholic school 11–12
    cultural standing of Sex
        Pistols 42–5
    dislike by fellow players 143
    'ever get the feeling you've been
        cheated?' 20, 108–9
    hippie movement 12–13
    hurt by Sid Vicious death 139–40
    insulting reporters 24
    Matlock, Glen 41
    musical interests 38–9
    original bands 45–6
    own philosophy 149
    pan-racial appeal of punk music 98–9
    power with the fans 44
    safety-pin style 17
    selling-out claims 53–4
    Sex Pistols reunion tour 2003: 158–60
    success after the Sex Pistols 144–9
    success as soloist 146–7
    talent 24–5
    Vicious, Sid, support 73
    Vicious, Sid, death 139–40
    Virgin Records 58
Lynott, Phil 52

Manhattan 128
Maslin, Mike 69
Mather, Bill 69
Matlock, Glen 15, 30–1, 36, 41, 52, 140,
    142–4
Matrixbest 53, 56, 68
McDonough, Jimmy 57
McKagan, Duff 142
McLaren, Malcolm
    activities after the Sex Pistols
        149–51
    all PR is good 130
    celebration of himself 125
    claims to have invented punk 18, 137

court case loss to Sex Pistol Residuals 152
cue cards 88–9
egomaniac 63
London mayoral contest 150
Lydon's views on 10–11, 41
manipulator extraordinaire 125
Meyer views on 56
music journalist interviews 49–50
nihilistic attitude to The Sex Pistols 60, 69
opinions of by band members 18, 74, 124–5, 132
relationship with Temple 69–70
secret filming 17–18
Sex [shop] 16–17, 23, 81, 91–2, 100
situationist approach 61
solo performer 150
support from Tudor-Pole 150–1
television advertising 50
Temple views on 58
Metal Box 146
Meyer, Russell Albion 53, 54–7, 63
Millington, Mary 64–7
Britain's most notorious woman 66
Miss Bohrloch 64
Mobbs, Nick 27
Morrison, Jim 40
Morris, Dennis 14, 40
Moss, Jerry 36, 46
Murray, Charles Shaar 11
'My Way' 115, 133

Neurotic Outsiders 142
Never Mind The Bollocks... Here's The Sex Pistols 56, 81, 117–19, 133
'New Rose' 28

New York Dolls 15, 23, 36, 40, 52, 130, 131, 136, 137
New, Steve 52, 143
Nine To Five 128
'No Feelings' 36
'No Future' 36
'No One is Innocent – A Punk Prayer By Ronnie Biggs' 51
Nolan, Jerry 64
Numan, Gary 45

Offspring 162
Old Grey Whistle Test, The 46
Oldman, Gary 138
100 Club 17, 26
'Only Anarchists Are Pretty' 68

Pandaemonium 151
Parsons, Dave 131
Peaks, Pandora 55
Performance 105–6, 136
Petty, Tom 151
Pink Floyd 38
Pirroni, Marco 15–16, 91–2, 121
Plasmatics, The 143
Playbirds, The 65
Pokrzywa, Bernie 69
Police, The 45
Pollitt, Tessa 45, 122–4, 137, 138–9
Pollock, Jackson 87
Pop, Iggy 40
Popeye 128
'Pretty Vacant' 25, 36, 103, 117
Price, Bill 49
Professionals, The 141, 142
Public Image Ltd 9, 13, 144–7
'Public Image' 146
punk
British word 137
confrontational look 26
Establishment as the enemy 26–7, 43–4
fashion 119
fear of punk appearance turning to hatred 121–2
first band 130
first single 28
getting involved 44
heroin 123–4
look 19
magenta and yellow sleeve design 118–19
McLaren claims invention 18, 137
Nazi symbols 26, 119–20
not spectator sport 44
only other film of substance 68
other movies 169–71
pan-racial appeal 98–9
rock 20, 32–3
Punk Rock Movie, The 46, 71

Queen 42
Queen Elizabeth 47, 102

Queen of the Blues 65
Queen's Golden Jubilee 160
Queen's Silver Jubilee 47, 57, 102
Qui A Tué Bambi? 109
Quilter, Mary 64

Radio London 48
Rae, David 69
Raincoats, The 45
Ramones, The 23, 35, 39, 130
Raw Power 40
Read, Sir John 31–3
Redglare, Rockets 72
Reid, Jamie 18, 47, 48, 85–8, 118–19, 134–5
Rhodes, Bernie 140
Rich Kids, The 143
Richards, Keith 122
Richmond, Sophie 95
Ritchie, John Simon 13, 75
Robertson, Sandy 49
Robinson, Michelle 76
Rocky Horror Show, The 67
Rooke, Pamela 'Jordan' 14, 16–17, 68, 91, 127, 135
'Rotten stare' 24
Rotten TV 148
Rotten: No Irish, No Blacks, No Dogs 147
Rotten, Johnny *see* Lydon, John

safety-pins style 17, 24, 35
Sailor 50
Sanchez, Roger 150
Scabies, Rat 52
secret filming 17–18
Segell, Michael 72
Sex Pistols
    A & M Records 36, 40, 46
    audience for 25–6
    BBC ban 47
    CBS 27
    chronology 173–86
    concern at hero worship 59–60
    cultural standing 42–5
    discography – selected albums 195–201
    discography – singles 187–93
    early days 23–51
    EMI 27–34, 36
    end as a group 20–3

film plans 21
filming 46
future 159–62
Heathrow misbehaviour 35–6
incarnation suggested 140
individuals should think for
    themselves concept 154
last show together 20–3
last UK show 57
national prominence 29–31
public attitude changes over 20 years
    157–8
reunion tour 1996: 142, 143, 146
reunion tour 2003: 142, 146, 158
swearing on television 29–31
timeline 173–86
US tour and maximum offence 58
Virgin records 46–7
who got swindled? 162
Sex Pistols Residuals 152
Sex [shop] 16–17, 23, 81, 91–2, 100
Shaka, Jah 144
Sham 69: 131
Sheridan, Simon 65–7
Sid and Nancy 67, 138, 148–9
Simonon, Paul 24–5, 144, 148
Siouxsie & The Banshees 26, 135
Sioux, Siouxsie 30, 121
situationism 61, 96, 100
Slade 61
Slade in Flame 61, 134
Slits, The 45, 122–3, 137, 138–9
Small Faces, The 41
Smith, Todd 76
So Alone 52
'Something Else' 104
Sorum, Matt 142
Speakeasy Club 46
Spinal Tap 154
Spungen, Deborah 71, 138
Spungen, Nancy
    backing vocals 52
    death 70–5
    dislike of 138–9
    mock striptease 83–4
    'most unlikeable person' 14
    Nauseating Nancy 63–4
    relationship with Sid Vicious 58
    suicide attempts 64
    'terrible' 13

Star Trek: The Motion Picture 128
'Staying Alive' 54
Stewart, Rod 41, 49, 60
Stiff Little Fingers 130
Stones, The 54
Strummer, Joe 144
Styrene, Poly 45
'Submission' 36
Sullivan, David 64–5
'Summer of Hate' 122
Superman II 128
'Swords Of A Thousand Men' 67

Taylor, John 142
Temple, Julien 47–8, 57, 59
    film structure 62
    film was to be expected 61
    filmography 167
    Great Rock 'n' Roll Swindle, The
        124–5, 128–9
    post-film activities 151–8
    relationship with McLaren 69–70
    secret filming 17–18
Tenpole Tudor 67
Thin Lizzy 52
Thomas, Chris 28, 49
Thomas, Jeremy 68
Thorne, Mike 28, 33–4
Thunders, Johnny 52, 130
Tobler, John 38
Today television show 29–31, 94–5
Tubeway Army 45
Tudor-Pole, Ed 55, 67, 82–3,
    110–11, 140–1, 142, 150–1

Up, Ari 123
Ure, Midge 143
U-Roy 145

Vérités Et Mensonges 128
Vermorel, Judy 37
Vicious White Kids, The 52
Vicious, Sid
    affection inspired 138
    appreciations by colleagues 139–40
    arrested for fighting 76
    arrested for murder of Spungen 70–7
    background 13–14
    bail money 75
    bass playing 36–7

best remembered song 115–16
charismatic figure 103
death 77, 116–17, 141
dislike of name Sid 37–8
drug dependence 22, 58, 64, 70,
    73–4, 103–4
drugs overdose 20–1
gentleness 13, 139
heroin addiction 58
Meyer views on 56–7
'My Way' 115–16
only solo UK show 52
pussycat in real life 132
relationship with Nancy Spungen
    58, 70
strong opinions 37
suicide attempt 75–6
trial for murder of Spungen 74–5
upbringing 40
views on having fun 39–40
Vigo: Passion For Life 151
Visitors, The 82

Walker, Andy 68
Walker, Jim 146
Warhol, Andy 124, 133
Warner Brothers 56, 141
Weller, Paul 143
Welles, Orson 44–5, 128
Wellington-Lloyd, Helen
    [Helen of Troy] 62, 81
Westwood, Vivienne 18–20, 28–9, 48,
    68, 92, 110, 119–21
What Makes Britain Great? 148
'What's In A Word' 140
Who Killed Bambi? [title for film script] 55–6
'Who Killed Bambi?' 55, 67,
    109, 110–11, 133, 140–1
Who, The 132
Willcox, Toyah 135
Wobble, Jah 10, 144, 145, 146
'Won't Get Fooled Again' 132
Wordle, John 146
World's End [shop] 120–1

X-Ray Spex 45

'You Need Hands' 94
Young Ones, The 105